eternal consciousness

eternal consciousness

JOHN S. DUNNE

University of Notre Dame Press

Notre Dame, Indiana

Manufactured in the United States of America

Library of Congress Cataloging-in-Publication Data

Dunne, John S., 1929–
Eternal consciousness / John S. Dunne.
p. cm.
Includes bibliographical references and index.
ISBN-13: 978-0-268-02610-3
ISBN-10: 0-268-02610-6
E-ISBN: 978-0-268-07776-1
1. Immortality—Christianity. 2. Future life—Christianity.
3. Spirituality. I. Title.
BT921.3.D86 2012
236'.21—dc23
2012008950

If there were no eternal consciousness in a man,

if at the foundation of all there lay only a wildly seething power

which writhing with obscure passions produced everything

that is great and everything that is insignificant,

if a bottomless void never satiated lay hidden beneath all—

what then would life be but despair?

—Søren Kierkegaard

contents

preface

"How quiet, peaceful, and solemn, not at all as I ran," says Prince Andre lying on the battlefield at Austerlitz in the title scene of Tolstoy's *War and Peace*, "not as we ran, shouting and fighting . . . how differently do those clouds glide across that lofty infinite sky! How was it I did not see that lofty sky before? And how happy I am to have found it at last! Yes! All is vanity, all falsehood except that infinite sky. There is nothing, nothing, but that. But even it does not exist, there is nothing but quiet and peace. Thank God! . . ."[1]

Experiencing peace in the midst of war, eternity in the midst of time, Prince Andre in *War and Peace* is an example of eternal consciousness. The actual phrase "eternal consciousness" is from Kierkegaard in the epigraph of this book, "If there were no eternal consciousness in a man . . . what then would life be but despair?"[2] I was originally going to call this book *A Tension of Essences*, a tension of war and peace, a tension of time and eternity. That phrase is from Albert Lord's two books on the singer of tales, the tension of essences in oral storytelling that allows the story to come out in different ways, happy ending and sad ending.[3] Calling the book *Eternal Consciousness* then resolves the tension in favor of peace and eternity. Yet the tension of essences is still there.

There is the tension, first of all, between war and peace. "We can know more than we can tell," as Michael Polanyi says.[4] In telling the story of war we can know more than war, we can know peace. I think of Dag Hammarskjöld's brochure for the Meditation Room at the UN, beginning "We all have within us a center of stillness surrounded by silence."[5] I spent several days in New York visiting the Meditation Room a few years ago. It is as though you can reenact there the experience of peace in the midst of war that is described in *War and Peace*, Prince Andre lying on the battlefield looking up into the sky. You can do it by dwelling in your "center of stillness surrounded by silence." Of course you don't need the Meditation Room to do it, you can do it just sitting quietly in a room. All our troubles, as Pascal says, stem from our inability to sit quietly in a room.[6]

Then there is the tension between time and eternity. There is at once a contrast and a connection. The contrast appears in Wittgenstein's saying, "If by eternity is understood not endless temporal duration but timelessness, then he lives eternally who lives in the present."[7] The connection appears in Plato's saying that time is "a changing image of eternity."[8] If we rub the two thoughts together, we get something more comprehensive than just living in the present. We get the idea of living in time as a whole, relating to the past and the future as well as the present, like Dag Hammarskjöld saying "For all that has been—Thanks! To all that shall be—Yes!"[9] If the "Thanks!" and "Yes!" can be taken as prayer, this means living in the Presence, not just in the present. So Prince Andre, lying on the battlefield and looking up into the sky, is not just in the present but in the Presence.

If we see time as a dimension, an inference drawn by Minkowski from Einstein's Special Theory of Relativity, we can also see matter as a dimension, an inference I believe we can draw from Einstein's General Theory of Relativity. That would have far-reaching implications for our image of ourselves as human beings. For it would mean that matter situates as well as being situated. It would mean the human brain situates the human mind. It would mean the human body situates the human soul. This view of the mind-body problem would contrast with the view that the mind = the brain and also with the view that brain processes cause thought processes. Spirit is not reducible to matter, I want to say, nor does matter cause spirit, but matter situates spirit, situates the events of the spirit, "the phenomenology of spirit" as Hegel calls it. *Matter situates events.*

If matter situates events, even events of the spirit, there is a mystery about those events. "We listen to our inmost selves," Martin Buber says, "and do not know which sea we hear murmuring."[10] What are those events? Presences, I will say, "real presences" as George Steiner calls them, the presence of others, our presence to ourselves, and the presence of God. Hegel goes from the presence of others to our presence to ourselves in his "phenomenology of spirit," but there is a further move, to come into the presence of God, as Saint Augustine does, going from his *Soliloquies* to his *Confessions.* This then for me is the integral phenomenology of spirit, to go from the presence of others to the presence of God by way of presence to self.

An inner landscape opening onto infinity—that is what comes to light, I believe, in our presence to ourselves. This inner landscape is what Gerard Manley Hopkins calls *inscape,* but the inscape of a human being opens onto infinity, as in Saint Augustine's words at the beginning of his *Confessions,* "our heart is restless until it rests in You."[11] If the human brain situates the human mind, it appears that one hemisphere of the brain situates words and the other situates music. Just as a right-hand glove fits on the left hand if you turn it inside out, so there is a musical inside of words and a verbal inside of music. The theme, the musical theme, is the verbal inside of music, and the inscape is the musical inside of words.

It is the nature of love, as Meister Eckhart says, to change us into the things we love.[12] The love of music changes us; the love of words changes us; the love of God changes us. It is the love of God that causes us to be "oned with God" as in the phrase "the cloud of unknowing in the which a soul is oned with God" and in the phrase "into the darkness with love."[13] And the great circle of love, "The love is from God and of God and towards God,"[14] answers the basic questions of a life, "Where do you come from?" and "Where are you going?" There is a far point on this circle in our lives and in our times, it seems, where love passes through loneliness. That seems to be the point where we are now in the circle dance of time.

To pass on from this far point, to close the circle, we have to become aware of the eternal. "The mass of men live lives of quiet desperation," Thoreau's saying,[15] seems to hold true where there is no awareness of the eternal in us. When we do become aware of the eternal, that awareness is eternal consciousness. I think again of the words of a Chinese grandmother to one of my students who had become frustrated trying to learn a difficult Chopin nocturne on the piano. "You must love the music, not master it," her Chinese grandmother told her. "Music must be treated as all things that are eternal, such as love and understanding, because it is these things that will carry us through the darkness of our lives and the death of our bodies to the moon of everlasting peace."

So music and love and understanding, these are "things that are eternal," "things that will carry us through the darkness of our lives and the death of our bodies to the moon of everlasting peace." Eternal life thus is the deeper life, the life of relatedness, a life of music and love and understanding, a life on this side of death that can carry us through to the other side. "The moon of everlasting peace" I take to be a metaphor, though in the village the Chinese grandmother came from the afterlife was thought to be on the moon. At any rate, if there is an eternal consciousness in us, there is hope rather than despair or quiet desperation. Faith is a combination of willingness and hope, willingness to die and yet hope to live, willingness to walk alone and yet hope to walk unalone.

I have included a song cycle at the end of the book where I go from "A Tension of Essences" to "Eternal Consciousness."

I have written music for it in the form of a theme with variations for voice and piano, the theme taken from a birdsong I once heard. At the very end I have "A Note on Mind and Matter," where I put forward again a mathematical interpretation of matter as a dimension.

"We can know more than we can tell"

We all have within us a center of stillness surrounded
by silence
—Dag Hammarskjöld

"I'm outside my heart, looking for the way back in."[1] These words from a story can describe a spiritual problem of our times. We are outside our heart, looking for the way back in. I believe it is because among the traditional three lives, action and contemplation and enjoyment, we have a life of action and a life of enjoyment but for the most part we are lacking a life of contemplation. And the dire consequence of this is that our city is a violent city. "We can know more than we can tell,"[2] Polanyi's principle, points the way back into our heart, I believe, and into the life of contemplation.

"Story is our only boat for sailing on the river of time," Ursula LeGuin says, "but in the great rapids and the winding shallows no boat is safe."[3] What we can tell is the story, but what we can know more than we can tell, I believe, is the relationship, the *I and it* of our lifework, the *I and thou* of our human relations, but over and above these our relationship with the transcendent, for instance, the "I in them and thou in me" of the Gospel (John 17:23). Contemplative life is in the relationship, and in that life "the great rapids and the winding shallows" are the ordeals of what has been called "the dark night of the soul." Speaking of these in his *Grammar of Assent,* Newman says "Such are the dealings of Wisdom with the elect soul,"[4] and indeed "the great rapids and the winding shallows" seem to belong to what we can know more than we can tell.

Sailing on the river of time and yet knowing "no boat is safe," we can know our own unknowing, even "the cloud of unknowing in the which a soul is oned with God,"[5] and we can understand our relationships in this way, realizing we are calling the unknown "thou," recognizing the mystery in others and in ourselves. We can know more than we can tell in telling the story, therefore, but it is not a knowing of knowing, like Aristotle's God or Hegel's absolute knowledge, but a knowing of unknowing, like the wisdom of Socrates or the "learned ignorance" of Nicolas of Cusa. And this knowing of unknowing is the knowing of the contemplative life.

"We all have within us a center of stillness surrounded by silence," Dag Hammarskjöld writes at the beginning of his brochure for the Meditation Room at the UN.[6] It is when we are in our center of stillness that we can know more than we can tell. Our center of stillness is like the quiet eye of a storm, or again it is like a quiet eye with which we can see, "the quiet eye" as Sylvia Shaw Judson says of seeing art, "the harvest of a quiet eye" as Wordsworth says of poetry.[7] Let us consider what we can know and what we can tell in our "center of stillness surrounded by silence."

Telling the Story

"What then is time?" Saint Augustine asks in his *Confessions.* "Provided that no one asks me, I know. If I want to explain it to an inquirer, I do not know."[8] That is an illustration of Polanyi's point, "we can know more than we can tell." The riddle of time, moreover, is the key to storytelling. For every notion of time there is a story or a way of storytelling. In his novel *Einstein's Dreams* Alan Lightman illustrates each notion of time that Einstein considers with a dream, a story, for instance time as a circle, Nietzsche's idea of "the eternal recurrence of the same events."[9] If we stay with Saint Augustine's thinking on time, we can end up like Heidegger asking "Am I my time?"[10] Although I want to answer "No, I am *in* my time," still the basic story, I think, is the life story, and the larger story of the world usually reflects the life story in a given era.

As the life story is told in our era, the problem is "being toward death," as Heidegger calls it, and the solution is "freedom toward death."[11] That is what a student of mine was discovering when he came to me and said "I've found it! I've found it!" and I said "What have you found?" and he replied "You accept death! And then you're free!" The freedom is freedom to live and to love. I believe that is the solution in Heidegger's *Being and Time* where he says "Our provisional aim is the Interpretation of *time* as the possible horizon of any understanding whatsoever of Being."[12] It is a viewpoint that means to contain all other possible views, as *Einstein's Dreams* contains many possible views of time. In fact, though, Heidegger is assuming "I am my time" and that is a point of view that excludes eternal life. If I *am* my time, then if I accept my death I become free toward death and free to live and to love, but eternal life is out of the question. If I am *in* my time, on the other hand, then the door is open to eternal life.

"So it is in you, my mind, that I measure periods of time," Saint Augustine says, and Heidegger concludes from that "I *am* my time."[13] If we say instead "I am *in* my time," it is still true, "it is in you, my mind, that I measure periods of time." If I am *in* my time, however, and I measure time in my mind, then if I come to an insight into time it will be an insight also into my mind, and vice-versa an insight into my mind will also be an insight into time. Insight into image, as the turning point of a life, I imagine to be something like "For all that has been—Thanks! To all that shall be—Yes!" at the turning point in Dag Hammarskjöld's diary.[14] This is like "You accept death! And then you're free!" And yet it is different. It is rather like "Thinking is thanking," the mystic saying Heidegger is always quoting in his later work.[15] "Thanks!" and "Yes!" is a way of accepting life and death, but it is acceptance in the form of prayer. There is hope in it that does not appear in simply accepting death and becoming free.

"Thanks!" and "Yes!" can describe a life story like that of "paradigmatic individuals," as Karl Jaspers describes them, Buddha and Socrates and Jesus,[16] a life of contemplation and action, a going into solitude to gain insight (contemplation) and a coming back into the human circle to share the insight with others (action). Let us consider that form of the life story to see if and how it transcends other historic forms of the story.

"Once upon a time," the time of storytelling, is transformed by "Thanks!" and "Yes!"—the past by "Thanks!" and the future by "Yes!" The transformed time of storytelling appears in the parables of Buddha and in the parables of Jesus. The transformation itself appears in the pattern of withdrawal and return that can be seen in the story of Buddha going into the forest to achieve enlightenment and then coming back to spend the rest of his life teaching, and also in the story of Jesus going into the desert after being baptized by John the Baptist and then coming back to teach and announce the kingdom of God. The withdrawal into solitude is a transcending of the times that allows Gotama to return as the Buddha and Jesus to return as the Christ. The withdrawal is into contemplation, the return into action. The withdrawal is a transcending of the times, the return a redeeming of the times.

There is courage in this withdrawal and return. "That is at bottom the only courage that is demanded of us: to have courage for the most strange, the most singular and the most inexplicable that we may encounter," Rilke says. "That mankind has in this sense been cowardly has done life endless harm; the experiences that are called 'visions,' the whole so-called 'spiritual world,' death, all those things that are so closely akin to us, have by daily parrying been so crowded out of life that the senses with which we could have grasped them are atrophied. To say nothing of God."[17] We have to have courage also to pass over and enter into the withdrawal and the return.

There are problems, though, in passing over, those that appear in "the quest of the historical Jesus."[18] We could speak likewise of "the quest of the historical Buddha" and "the quest of the historical Socrates." A quest of certainty inevitably defeats itself, I think, for as we try to make sure we become ever more unsure. A quest of understanding is the way, I believe, for as we seek insight we go from one insight to another. Certainty is knowing we know; understanding is simply knowing. A Socratic knowing of our unknowing is an analogue of certainty on the way of understanding. A quest of understanding, I believe, enables us to pass over and to enter into the enlightenment that occurs in the solitude of the forest or to enter into the revelation that occurs in the solitude of the desert.

Indeed it may be that going over from the quest of certainty to the quest of understanding is the very turn that yields enlightenment and revelation. Let us try this as a way of passing over to enlightenment and then as a way of passing over to revelation, keeping in mind "we can know more than we can tell." It is true, this may be like Peter Matthiessen's quest in *The Snow Leopard.* He finds the tracks of the Snow Leopard, but he never sees the Snow Leopard itself. We may find the tracks to enlightenment without coming to enlightenment, and we may find the tracks to revelation without coming to revelation. For the tracks are what we can tell, but the enlightenment and the revelation are what we can know more than we can tell.

Years ago I was moved by the simplicity of Henry Clarke Warren's summary of the life of Gotama the Buddha, how in the forest "he became illumined and saw the Great Truths" and how his "first aim had been merely his own salvation; but moved by pity for mankind he resolved to bestow on others the Four Great Truths and the eight-fold path."[19] I saw Gotama's life story simply as one of gaining and sharing insight, and I thought of the parallel with the life of Jesus, Gotama going into the forest and Jesus going into the desert, Gotama coming back into the human circle to share his insight with others and Jesus likewise coming back to spend his life teaching others. To be sure, Gotama's life is much longer than the life of Jesus, and yet both show the pattern of withdrawal and return. Now the question is whether we can understand the illumining that occurs in solitude and is shared in the human circle as essentially a going from certainty to understanding.

"No self" (*anatta*) seems to be the heart of the Four Great Truths: "all egocentric life is suffering; this suffering is caused by misknowing and its consequences; there is a real freedom from this suffering; the path to that freedom is eightfold" (Robert Thurman's formulation).[20] To pass over to this from a Western standpoint seems to mean passing over from a quest of certainty where "I think therefore I am" to a quest of understanding. There is a connection between self and certainty, as in "I think therefore I am," and likewise a connection between "no self" (*anatta*) and understanding as enlightenment. I want to say, however, that it is not certainty that is being abandoned here but the quest of certainty, and so too it is not selfhood that is being abandoned but self in quest of certainty. For there is another quest that is being affirmed here, the quest of understanding, and so we could even say the self in quest of understanding is being affirmed here.

Here now I may have found the tracks of the Snow Leopard but not yet seen the Snow Leopard itself. I may be on the path to enlightenment, that is, having abandoned the quest of certainty and the self in quest of certainty, but have not yet abandoned the quest of understanding and the self in quest of understanding. "I would like to see a snow leopard, but if I do not, that is all right, too," Peter Matthiessen says in *The Snow Leopard,* and "When you are ready, Buddhists say, the teacher will appear. In the way he (Tukten) watched me, in the way he smiled, he was awaiting me; had I been ready, he might have led me far enough along the path 'to see the snow leopard.'"[21] I think of the last word of Gotama to his disciples, "Walk on!"[22]

Writing about "the Sense of 'I' in Christianity," I made a distinction between self as will and self as our "center of stillness surrounded by silence."[23] I took the "no self" doctrine of Buddhism and the loss of self in Alzheimer's disease to be no self as will and the loss of self as will, leaving the deep self intact as "center of stillness surrounded by silence." I still want to maintain that, passing over to Buddhism and coming back again to my roots in Christianity. It may mean that my passing over to Buddhism is necessarily incomplete, as I follow Christ rather than Buddha. All the same, I gain some insight into Buddhism by going over from the quest of certainty to the quest of understanding.

Passing over to Christ also requires a going over from a quest of certainty to a quest of understanding insofar as doubt is the heart of a quest of certainty and faith is the heart of a quest of understanding. What I mean is when I try to make sure and become ever more unsure, I am following a path of doubt. When I seek insight and go with whatever little light I have, I am following a path of faith. Albert Schweitzer in his *Quest of the Historical Jesus* seems to take both paths—in the body of the work the path of doubt ending in what he calls "thoroughgoing skepticism and eschatology," but in the last paragraph the path of faith, saying "And to those who obey Him, whether they be wise or simple, He will reveal Himself in the toils, the conflicts, the sufferings which they shall pass through in His fellowship, and, as an ineffable mystery, they shall learn in their own experience Who He is."[24]

Now "Thanks!" and "Yes!" means going over from self as will to self as willingness, and thus opening up to the deeper self "we all have within us," "a center of stillness surrounded by silence." This is not exactly "no self" (*anatta*) as in Buddhism but it is what has been called "self-transcendence."[25] The turning points in the life of Jesus, going into solitude, coming back into the human circle, and facing death, seem to reflect the self-transcendence of "Thanks!" and "Yes!" There is the "You are" of his baptism by John the Baptist ("You are my beloved Son, in whom I am well pleased" Mark 1:11) and the

"Are you?" of his temptations in the loneliness of the desert ("If you are the Son of God . . ."). This is the first great turning point of his life, a point where he himself seems to learn, "as an ineffable mystery," in his own experience in solitude "Who He is."

Coming back into the human circle, the second great turning point, Jesus begins to teach, saying "The time is fulfilled, and the kingdom of God is at hand" (Mark 1:15). From the viewpoint of "thoroughgoing skepticism and eschatology" this means the end of the world, something that has not happened. If we take the path of faith, though, instead of the path of doubt, then the message of Jesus to us is the same as to the original disciples, "Follow me!" Thus Schweitzer, taking the path of faith after walking the path of doubt to the end, concludes "He comes to us as One unknown, without a name, as of old, by the lake-side, He came to those men who knew Him not. He speaks to us the same word: Follow thou me! and sets us to the tasks which He has to fulfil for our time. He commands. . . ."[26]

Facing death then, the third great turning point, Jesus goes through death to life, according to the Gospels. Telling the story from the viewpoint of "thoroughgoing skepticism and eschatology," Schweitzer writes,

There is silence all around. The Baptist appears, and cries: "Repent, for the Kingdom of Heaven is at hand." Soon after that comes Jesus, and in the knowledge that He is the coming Son of Man lays hold of the wheel of the world to set it moving on that last revolution which is to bring all ordinary history to a close. It refuses to turn, and He throws Himself upon it. Then it does turn; and crushes Him. Instead of bringing in the eschatological conditions, He has destroyed them. The wheel rolls onward, and the mangled body of the one immeasurably great Man who was strong enough to think of Himself as the spiritual ruler of mankind and to bend history to His purpose, is hanging upon it still. That is His victory and His reign.[27]

Telling the story from the standpoint of faith, on the other hand, he writes, as we have been quoting him,

> He comes to us as One unknown, without a name, as of old, by the lake-side, He came to those men who knew Him not. He speaks to us the same word: "Follow thou me!" and sets us to the tasks which He has to fulfil for our time. He commands. And to those who obey Him, whether they be wise or simple, He will reveal Himself in the toils, the conflicts, the sufferings which they shall pass through in His fellowship, and, as an ineffable mystery, they shall learn in their own experience Who He is.[28]

Observe how the story becomes present rather than simply past, from the standpoint of faith, and how the New Testament word for presence is *parousia*, meaning "presence" and "coming," as if to say "I am with you always, even unto the end of time" (Matthew 28:20). He is present among us now, but in the end his presence will become manifest.

Withdrawal and return, therefore, as in the life of Gotama and in the life of Jesus, constitute a story of transcending and transforming time. Presence, the *parousia* of Jesus present and coming, is the answer to death in his story, the presence of God-with-us. "You are a councillor: if you can command these elements to silence and work *the peace of the present*, we will not hand a rope more; use your authority," the Boatswain says to Gonzalo in Shakespeare's *Tempest*. "If you cannot, give thanks you have lived so long, and make yourself ready in your cabin for the mischance of the hour, if it so hap—Cheerly, good hearts!—Out of our way, I say."[29] Peace of the present, or better, peace of the presence is the answer to death, peace of the present in Buddhism, peace of the presence in Christianity.

"Calming the storm," as my sister describes "exercises leading to contemplation,"[30] is working the peace of the present or working the peace of the presence. "If by eternity is understood not endless temporal duration but timelessness, then he lives eternally who lives in the present," Wittgenstein says, or in another translation, "eternal life belongs to those who live in the present."[31] I want to say instead *eternal life belongs to those who live in the presence.* In Buddhist meditation eternal life is found in living in the present; in Christian prayer eternal life is found in living in the presence. The story of Jesus calming the storm (Matthew 8:24–27, Mark 4:37–41, Luke 8:23–25), if we compare it with the story of him walking on the water (Matthew 14:24–33, Mark 6:47–51, John 6:16–21), is a story of the Shekinah, the presence ("It is I," that is "I am"). As an exercise leading to contemplation, calming the storm means entering into our "center of stillness surrounded by silence."

I want to take the surrounding silence as the surrounding presence of God. "Where the storyteller is loyal, eternally and unswervingly loyal to the story, there, in the end, silence will speak," Isak Dinesen says in one of her stories. "Where the story has been betrayed, silence is but emptiness."[32] Telling the story of Jesus, his withdrawal and return, his going through death to life, from the standpoint of faith, allows the silence to speak of the divine presence. Telling the story from the standpoint of "thoroughgoing skepticism and eschatology," on the other hand, leaves the silence empty. It is true, the silence is simply silence also in Buddhist meditation, and yet the silence speaks. "Who then tells a finer tale than any of us?" Isak Dinesen continues. "Silence does. And where does one read a deeper tale than upon the more perfectly printed page of the most precious book? Upon the blank page." And that is the name of this story of hers, "The Blank Page." "Whereof one cannot speak," Wittgenstein ends in his *Tractatus,* "thereof one must be silent."[33]

Telling my own story then from the standpoint of faith seeking understanding, I can tell it too as a story of gaining and sharing insight. Aging and loneliness, the main issues of my life, become occasions of insight, but is insight enough? Aging raises the problem of death, and insight here for me is coming to a sense of eternal life. And loneliness raises the problem of love, and insight here for me is coming to a vision of the great circle, "The love is from God, and of God, and towards God."[34] Love and death then lead me to a vision of the great circle of life and light and love, as in the Gospel of John, and to a faith in God-with-us. If "we can know more than we can tell" and if we can tell of the great circle, what then can we know of life and light and love?

Knowing the Relationship

"Only connect!" E. M. Forster says in *Howard's End*, and the connection, the relationship, is what we can know more than we can tell. "Only connect the prose and the passion," Forster says, "and both will be exalted, and human love will be seen at its height. Live in fragments no longer. Only connect, and the beast and the monk, robbed of the isolation that is life to either, will die."[35] Withdrawal and return, nevertheless, the pattern we found in the life of Gotama and in the life of Jesus, is not the same as living in fragments or in isolation, but is a connecting with transcendence as well as with human existence. "It may be that a clear sense of the self can only crystallize round something transcendental," Robert Bolt says, thinking of Saint Thomas More.[36] It may be too that a clear sense of "no self" (*anatta*) can only crystallize round something transcendental, as we go beyond self as will to willingness and the deep center of stillness we have within us.

"As God is one," Newman says, "so the impression which He gives us of Himself is one."[37] I gather that it is an impression of presence, of "I am with you," of companionship on the journey of life. In Christianity it is the impression of "God-with-us." If "we all have within us a center of stillness surrounded by silence," I want to take the surrounding silence, as I have said, to be the surrounding presence of God. We can know more than we can tell, Polanyi explains, by dwelling in the particulars of what we know. Our dwelling in the particulars of our life, a phrase in Shakespeare, "the particulars of my life," is the other side, it seems to me, of God dwelling in us.

"Do thou stand for my father," Prince Hal says to Falstaff, "and examine me on the particulars of my life."[38] Saint Augustine's prayer in his *Soliloquies*, "May I know me! May I know thee!"[39] suggests the connection between my indwelling in the particulars of my life and God's indwelling in me.

"I in them, and thou in me," the formula in the Gospel of John (John 17:23), makes a similar connection between Christ dwelling in those who follow him and God dwelling in Christ. God's presence to us, I gather, is the other side of our presence to ourselves. We cannot jump over our own shadow. We are a mystery to ourselves, that is, and that is the other side of the mystery God is to us. "May I know me! May I know thee!" is the prayer, therefore, and the question of our presence to ourselves and God's presence to us. Deconstruction, the work of Paul DeMan and Jacques Derrida, is an attempt to undo "the metaphysics of presence." *Real Presences* by George Steiner is an answer.[40] Our presence to ourselves and God's presence to us, I believe, are the principal instances. We can know more than we can tell of our presence to ourselves and God's presence to us by dwelling in the particulars of our life.

"Our relation to our fellow men is that of prayer," Kafka says, "our relation to ourselves, that of effort, from prayer we draw the strength for effort."[41] Another translation for "effort" here is "striving." It is also possible to go from effort or striving to prayer in relation to ourselves. Let us consider what it means to go from effort or striving to prayer in relation to others, and to ourselves, and to God.

"Even if Kafka did not pray—and this we do not know," Walter Benjamin says, "he still possessed in the highest degree what Malebranche called 'the natural prayer of the soul': attentiveness."[42] Our relation to our fellow humans is one of prayer, I take it, because we are unable to control one another, to make one another feel or think or do what we want. Thus we are a mystery to one another, and to recognize the mystery, the unknown and uncontrollable, is like prayer, or at least like attentiveness, "the natural prayer of the soul." We do think we are able to control ourselves, on the other hand, "to conquer myself rather than fortune," as Descartes said,[43] but we may come to realize we are a mystery also to ourselves, that we cannot leap over our own shadow. Then our relation to ourselves too becomes one of prayer instead of striving. "Attention is the natural prayer of the soul," as Malebranche says, and attention means recognizing the mystery in others and in ourselves. When we go from striving to prayer we come to a kind of peace with others and with ourselves.

I and thou, as Martin Buber describes it, seems to mean this attention, this peace, this recognition of mystery in the other and in myself. Goethe and Socrates and Jesus are the figures Buber singles out to illustrate the *I and thou* relationship, Goethe for his relationship with nature, Socrates for dialogue, and Jesus for his relationship with God. "And to anticipate by taking an illustration from the realm of unconditional relation: how powerful, even to being overpowering, and how legitimate, even to being self-evident, is the saying of *I* by Jesus!" he says. "For it is the *I* of unconditional relation in which the man calls his *Thou* Father in such a way that he himself is simply Son, and nothing else but Son."[44] Buber concludes, nevertheless, that the relationship can be universal, "every man can say *Thou* and is then *I*, every man can say Father and is then Son."

I want to say it can be universal but by way of indwelling, as in the formula in John 17:23, *I in them and thou in me*. Indwelling is the thing Buber is rejecting in this same passage where he says "It is useless to limit this *I* to a power in itself or this *Thou* to something dwelling in ourselves, and once again to empty the real, the present relation, of reality." Yet dwelling in the particulars of our life is how we can know more than we can tell. And our dwelling in the particulars of our life is the other side of God dwelling in us. That seems to be the secret of what is called "the practice of the presence of God."[45] Brother Lawrence, picking up straws for God, dwelling thus in the particulars of his life, was practising the presence of God, living in the presence of God dwelling in us.

There is an intentionality, a purposiveness, in picking up straws *for God*, to be sure, and that intentionality does amount to living in the presence of God. It is like the intentionality in "abandonment to divine providence," *l'abandon* that is described by Jean-Pierre de Caussade.[46] It is a dwelling in the particulars of one's life with the thought of giving oneself over to the will of God. Dwelling is thinking, as Heidegger says, and thinking is thanking. It is a dwelling that is thinking and a thinking that is thanking by which we can know more than we can tell. "The practice of the presence of God" and "abandonment to divine providence" comes out of a "Thanks!" and a "Yes!" to the particulars of a life, a "Thanks!" for the past, a "Yes!" to the future.

Waiting on God, Simone Weil's concept of *attente de Dieu*, is like Malebranche's "attention is the natural prayer of the soul." "The key to a Christian conception of studies is the realization that prayer consists of attention," she says. "It is the orientation of all the attention of which the soul is capable toward God. The quality of the attention counts for much in the quality of prayer. Warmth of heart cannot make up for it."[47] Actually this seems close to a Rabbinic concept of studies as learning to love God with all your mind. I think also of Saint Thomas Aquinas saying prayer is an act of the intellect.[48] Dwelling in the particulars of your life can become prayer, as it is for Saint Augustine in his *Confessions*. As Goethe thinks of his life in terms of truth and poetry, turning the truth of his life into poetry, Saint Augustine thinks of his life in terms of truth and prayer, turning the truth of his life into prayer.

"From prayer we draw the strength for effort," Kafka says, and that seems to hold true even where the relationship is essentially one of prayer. "Walk on!" But we draw the strength to walk on from prayer. A journey with God in time is essentially a relationship where from prayer we draw the strength to walk on. I am thinking of times of depression when we are dispirited or dejected. It is then that "Walk on!" becomes the guiding imperative of a life. I think of Newman's prayer,

Lead, kindly light,
Amid the encircling gloom

Lead Thou me on!
The night is dark,
And I am far from home—
Lead Thou me on!
Keep Thou my feet;
I do not ask to see
The distant scene—
One step enough for me.[49]

Newman wrote these lines as a young man, recovering from a fever while he was in Sicily. "My servant thought that I was dying, and begged for my last directions," he writes. "I gave them as he wished; but I said, 'I shall not die'. I repeated 'I shall not die, for I have not sinned against the light. I have not sinned against the light'. I never have been able quite to make out what I meant."[50] Whatever he meant, he had the image of light in mind, and so when he wrote the lines "Lead, kindly light" he was thinking of God as light, as "kindly light." He was drawing from prayer the strength to walk on, "Lead Thou me on!" There may even be a deeper connection here, as in Tolstoy's story of Ivan Ilych facing death, "In place of death there was light."[51]

What Newman says of the "kindly light" is very close to what Saint Augustine says of the inner teacher and the doctrine of illumination. This idea that Christ is the inner teacher does appeal to me in my experience of teaching, for I find myself praying that God will work in the minds and hearts of my students, and thinking that even when a lecture is a failure or a partial failure, the inner teacher working in minds and hearts can turn the failure into success. The idea is close also to the Quaker doctrine of the inner light that gives enlightenment and guidance and assurance. It speaks also to the problem of death, as in Newman's words "I shall not die. I have not sinned against the light," or more clearly in Tolstoy's words, "In place of death there was light."

"May it be a light to you in dark places, when all other lights go out," Tolkien has Galadriel say to Frodo, giving him a phial of light.[52] That phrase, *a light when all other lights go out*, seems to be a description also of the inner light, the kindly light that enables you to walk on. It is indeed "a light to you in dark places." It could be said also of a guiding image, like the image of your life as a journey in time, or even more, like that of a journey with God in time. Here the image is very close to the inner reality of a guiding light. I think of something a friend of mine told me, how the image of her life as a journey in time was a guiding light in her recovery from cancer. The image and the inner light seem related as insight into image. We can know more than we can tell in telling our story as a journey in time, knowing the relationship with God that makes it a journey with God in time.

When we tell our story from a rhetorical standpoint before others, like Newman in his *Apologia,* we can know more than we can tell insofar as we can know our story also from a meditative standpoint before self and a contemplative standpoint before God. Newman speaks of his relation with God there in his *Apologia* and describes it as *solus cum Solo,* "alone with the Alone,"[53] showing that he was aware of the meditative standpoint before self and the contemplative standpoint before God, and yet he is speaking there always from the rhetorical standpoint before others.

When we tell our story from a meditative standpoint before self, like Marcus Aurelius in his *Meditations* or Saint Augustine in his *Soliloquies,* we can know more than we can tell insofar as we can know our story also from a contemplative standpoint before God. At any rate, Saint Augustine seems to have a glimpse of that standpoint before God in his short prayer in the *Soliloquies,* "May I know me! May I know thee!" That short prayer leads into the sustained prayer of his *Confessions.* Marcus Aurelius, on the other hand, with his "inner citadel," as Pierre Hadot calls it,[54] may not be open to anything further.

When we tell our story then from a contemplative standpoint before God, like Saint Augustine in his *Confessions,* is it still true to say "we can know more than we can tell" or are we telling all? If our relationship to others is one of prayer, as

Kafka says, and our relationship to ourselves is one of effort but from prayer we draw the strength for effort, our relationship also to ourselves is one of prayer, as we have seen, and so we recognize the mystery in others and in ourselves. So telling our story from a contemplative standpoint before God involves a recognition of mystery in others and in ourselves. "May I know you, who know me," Saint Augustine prays in his *Confessions*,[55] as if the prayer of his *Soliloquies* still holds good, "May I know me! May I know thee!" There is more than we can tell, therefore, and we can know there is more.

"Short prayer penetrates heaven," it is said in *The Cloud of Unknowing*.[56] And these short prayers, "May I know me! May I know thee!" and "May I know you, who know me," are for me a more accessible model of contemplative prayer than the sustained prayer of the *Confessions*. Also Kafka's remark, "Our relation to our fellow men is that of prayer, our relation to ourselves that of effort; from prayer we draw the strength for effort," is for me a guiding insight along with the imperative "Walk on!" If I envision my life as a journey in time and, taking into account the deep loneliness of the human condition, a journey with God in time, and seeing "time as the possible horizon for any understanding whatsoever of Being," I may see walking with God as an answer to death, "And Enoch walked with God: and he was not; for God took him" (Genesis 5:24).

Telling the story like this, he "walked with God, and he was not, for God took him," is telling it in terms of the relationship with God. If we make a distinction between what we can tell and what we can know, the story is what we can tell and the relationship is what we can know. So if we tell the story in terms of the relationship, the story can appear to be a legend. All the same, we *can* know the relationship, but that knowing is a knowing of our unknowing, as in "the cloud of unknowing in the which a soul is oned with God." Thus in telling the story of the Gospels, Albert Schweitzer comes to "thoroughgoing skepticism and eschatology," and yet ends in faith with "He comes to us as One unknown. . . ." Perhaps the solution is *distinguer pour unir*, to distinguish in order to unite.

"A kind of mysticism emerges as champion in a field abandoned by learning and critical reasoning," it has been said of Schweitzer's conclusion.[57] If the mysticism is that of "the cloud of unknowing in the which a soul is oned with God," however, it is not uncritical. We can know more than we can tell, but that knowing is in virtue of a relationship, an *I and thou*, really an *I in them and thou in me*. So one who would accept only "learning and critical reasoning," but would stand outside the relationship, could not accept the conclusion, "He comes to us as One unknown . . . He speaks to us the same word: Follow thou me! . . . And to those who obey Him, whether they be wise or simple, He will reveal Himself . . . and, as an ineffable mystery, they shall learn in their own experience Who He is."

A union or communion with ultimate reality, that is the usual definition of mysticism, and that union or communion is where the higher religions seem to agree or converge. I think of Rudolf Otto's essay, *Mysticism East and West*, comparing Sankara from the East and Meister Eckhart from the West.[58] The formula of union or communion with ultimate reality that I have been using here is that of the Gospel of John 17:23, *I in them and thou in me*. We can know more than we can tell in telling the Christian story if we know the indwelling of Christ in us, *I in them*, and the indwelling of God in Christ, *and thou in me*. So also in telling our own story, we can tell of our journey in time but we can know of God-with-us on the journey.

Is Matter a Dimension?

Everything that exists is situated. Everything that's above matter is situated; matter itself is situated.
—Max Jacob

Space is three-dimensional, and time is a fourth dimension, and matter is thought to be situated in space and time. If we say matter itself is a dimension, though, then what is situated in space and time and matter? Events? Let us say matter *is* a dimension along with space and time, and let us say *events* are what are situated in space and time and matter, and let us see where this leads us. Telling a story then, as we have been doing, is telling of events in space and time and matter. "A story that is to be told," Padraic Colum says, "has to be about happenings."[1]

"Everything that exists is situated," Max Jacob says. "Everything that's above matter is situated; matter itself is situated."[2] If we say matter is a dimension, though, then matter *situates* as well as being situated. That would mean the brain situates the mind, the body situates the soul, and generally matter situates events or happenings of all kinds. I think of Einstein's theory of relativity. His original theory, the special theory of relativity (1905), led to Minkowski's inference that time is a dimension. His later theory, the general theory of relativity (1915), I believe, could lead to a similar inference that matter is a dimension. There has been a renaissance of general relativity in our time, and so perhaps it is time to draw this inference from the curvature of space and time that arises from matter in general relativity.

If matter is a dimension along with space and time, then storytelling is about spirit. I think of Heinrich von Kleist's marvelous essay "On the Marionette Theatre" where he speaks of "the path taken by the soul of the dancer."[3] The marionette, as he describes it, is a doll suspended by a string attached to its center of gravity. It is an image of the dancer. But "the path taken by the soul of the dancer" is the path of the spirit. The story of the spirit then goes from unconscious unity with the body and on through partial consciousness to full consciousness. Grace as gracefulness is there in the beginning and in the end, but it is missing in the partial consciousness of the middle. In the beginning and in the end we are as graceful as dancers, but we lack that grace now in the middle time.

"Grace appears most purely in the human form which either has no consciousness or an infinite consciousness," the dancer says in Kleist's essay. "Does that mean," Kleist answers, "we must eat again of the tree of knowledge in order to return to the state of innocence?" "Of course," the dancer replies, "but that's the final chapter in the history of the world."[4] If we say matter situates the spirit, then the brain situates the consciousness, and the body situates the soul of the dancer.

Does the Brain Situate the Mind?

"This is the point where the two ends of the circular world meet," the dancer says to Kleist, speaking of conscious and unconscious grace.[5] The relation of body and mind, according to this, is a circle, going from unconscious to conscious unity by way of partial consciousness with its separation of body and mind. If we speak then of the brain and the mind, we come upon this circle and this same "point where the two ends of the circular world meet." I think of the two hemispheres of the brain, and how words are associated with the left hemisphere and music with the right hemisphere, and how there seems to have been an original unity of words and music, as in Vico's idea that "the world's first languages were in song,"[6] and thus perhaps an ultimate unity or harmony to come which I want to call "the music of words."

Now the right hemisphere seems to be connected to the left hand and the left hemisphere to the right hand. So if a person suffers a stroke in the right hemisphere, as happened to a friend of mine, the paralysis occurs in the left hand and the left leg. I noticed that my friend, who was fifty years old or so, was still able to speak, but her speech at first was in a high monotone. Her speech lacked what is called "the speech melody," the rise and fall in pitch that occurs in normal speech. As she recovered from the stroke, the speech melody came back and her voice began to sound normal again. The connection with the left hand and the left leg has remained a problem, though, as if the recovery has never been quite complete.

Speaking to "the Kantian problem of the right and left hand which cannot be made to cover one another," Wittgenstein says "A right hand glove could be put on a left hand if it could be turned round in four-dimensional space."[7] Actually it seems to me there is a simpler solution: a right hand glove could be put on a left hand if it could be turned inside out. Thus too, if words are associated with the left hemisphere and the right hand, and music is associated with the right hemisphere and the left hand, then words are music inside out, as it were, and music words inside out. I am right handed myself, and I have thought of words as my right hand, my stronger side, and music as my left hand, my weaker side. All the same, the real relation between words and music seems congruent to the relation between the two hemispheres of the brain.

To be sure, I know much more about words and music than I do about the two hemispheres of the brain. If we can assume, nevertheless, that one hemisphere situates words and the other hemisphere situates music, then we can indeed say the brain does situate the mind.

"Paradise is locked and bolted," the dancer says to Kleist, "now that we've eaten of the tree of knowledge, and the cherubim stand behind us. We have to go on now and make the journey round the world to see if it is perhaps open somewhere at the back."[8] This is the circular journey to the point where the two ends of the circular world meet. We have to grow into full consciousness, that is, to overcome the effects of our partial consciousness. How? Hegel thought to accomplish this in his *Phenomenology of Spirit* by going from our usual standpoint before others to the inner standpoint before self. I am thinking it is accomplished by going on from the standpoint before self, like that of Saint Augustine in his *Soliloquies*, to the standpoint before God, like that in his *Confessions*. The key, I imagine, is in his prayer in the *Soliloquies*, "May I know me! May I know thee!" that leads on into the sustained prayer of his *Confessions*. I think this may be the back entrance into paradise that Kleist's dancer was seeking.

"While I was speaking to him I did not know what was going on in his head," Wittgenstein quotes from ordinary conversation. "In saying this," he comments, "one is not thinking of brain processes, but of thought processes."[9] So he makes a distinction between "brain processes" and "thought processes." If we can make a similar distinction between the things of life and our relation to the things of life, we can suppose that brain processes have to do with the things of life and thought processes have to do with our relation to the things of life. The "phenomenology of spirit" then, as Hegel calls it, is the story of our relation to the things of life. Hegel's concept of spirit, nevertheless, as "pure self-identity within otherness,"[10] takes the story only from the standpoint before others to the standpoint before self. We have to make a further move to the standpoint before God to find the back door to paradise.

If we suppose brain processes have to do with the things of life and thought processes have to do with our relation to the things of life, then it is our thought processes that *interpret* the words and music of our brain processes. Our story and our song have a structure in our brain processes, but they get an interpretation in our thought processes. Newman tells his story in his *Apologia,* but he tells it from a rhetorical standpoint before others, answering criticisms and attacks on his integrity. The standpoint before others is a relationship to the story and it is an interpretation. So too is the meditative standpoint before self in the *Meditations* of Marcus Aurelius and the *Soliloquies* of Saint Augustine, and so too is the contemplative standpoint before God in the *Confessions* of Saint Augustine.

Our relation to the things of life is manifold, to be sure, not just the overall relations we have mentioned, before others, before self, before God. All the same, these overall relations can unify our life, especially that before self and that before God, as in Kafka's saying, "Our relation to our fellow men is that of prayer, our relation to ourselves, that of effort, from prayer we draw the strength for effort." This unity of relationship may tell us something about the unity between the verbal and the musical sides of the brain. I think of the definition of song Saint Thomas Aquinas gives in his preface to the Psalms, "Song is the leap of mind in the eternal breaking out into sound."[11]

Song unifies the verbal and the musical sides of the brain, and if we think of it as "the leap of mind in the eternal breaking out into sound," it expresses the mind's unifying contemplative standpoint before God. I think of Stravinsky's *Symphony of Psalms,* drawing on three of the Psalms (39, 40, and 150), or Saint Augustine's *Confessions,* drawing also especially on three Psalms (4, 42, and 139), though not set to music. Looking at the definition of song more closely, we find three elements:

exultatio mentis	the leap of mind
de aeternis habita	in the eternal
prorumpens in vocem	breaking out into sound

The leap of mind is actually *exultatio mentis,* an exultation of the mind, a joyous transport, *de aeternis habita,* over eternal things, *prorumpens in vocem,* breaking out into sound or into voice. If the brain situates the mind, what does this tell us about the brain and what does it tell us about the mind?

A somewhat similar and yet somewhat different question has been posed by neuroscientists. "As far as we know, humans are the only species that synchronize to a beat, that move or tap their feet to musical rhythms," Ani Patel says. "What does that tell us about the human brain and its structure and function?"[12] Rhythm is the element that is common to words and music. I think of Saint Augustine writing *On Music* and of a song I wrote to him called "Unchanging Number":

> Tell me, Master
> how you turn
> from changing to unchanging number
> and are sensible to
> music of eternal life,
> or tell me rather how to listen
> to unchanging number in the changing
> and to hear eternal music
> in the song of earth.[13]

Here I have brought the discussion back to song as "the leap of mind in the eternal breaking out into sound."

I think of *The Songlines* by Bruce Chatwin,[14] about the aboriginal pathways across Australia, and I wonder if song is related to journey, to journey in time for us who are no longer aboriginal nomads. I wonder too if song is related to a journey with God in time, as I envision my own life, and if that is how song is "the leap of mind in the eternal breaking out into sound." I found to my own surprise that the voyages and travels of my own life largely ceased when I returned to music and began to compose song cycles and song and dance cycles, as if music somehow took the place of the voyages and travels, or as if music were itself voyage and travel.

Number, changing and unchanging, as Saint Augustine speaks of it in his essay *On Music,* is the rhythm that is common to words and music. There are all the different ways of responding to music that E. M. Forster speaks of in *Howard's End,* "Whether you are like Mrs. Munt, and tap surreptitiously when the tunes come—of course, not so as to disturb others—; or like Helen, who can see heroes and shipwrecks in the music's flood; or like Margaret, who can only see the music; or like Tibby, who is profoundly versed in counterpoint, and holds the full score open on his knee. . . ."[15] If we follow "the path taken by the soul of the dancer," however, the path of the spirit, we are led, as I say in my song, "to hear eternal music in the song of earth."

If the brain does situate the mind, then we can expect the song of earth to situate eternal music. What I mean is something like Plato saying time is "a changing image of eternity."[16] The music of time, thus, is a changing image of eternal music. If we make a distinction between the person and the life that the person lives, saying the person is like a vertical dimension passing through the horizontal dimension of the life, the changing image of eternity is the changing image of the person passing through the life. The song of earth then is about the life, the life story or part of the life story, while eternal music is about the person. "For within our whole universe the story only has authority to answer that cry of heart of its characters, that one cry of heart of each of them: *Who am I?*" as Isak Dinesen says in the first of her *Last Tales.*[17] The song of earth is to eternal music, I am thinking, as the story is to the cry of heart, *Who am I?*

An eternal consciousness is the answer to the cry of the heart, according to Kierkegaard. "If there were no eternal consciousness in a man," he says in *Fear and Trembling,* "if at the foundation of all there lay only a wildly seething power which writhing with obscure passions produced everything that is great and everything that is insignificant, if a bottomless void never satiated lay hidden beneath all—what then would life be but despair?"[18] This eternal consciousness, nevertheless, is extended in time, in a journey in time, and so the life story tells us who we are. If the brain were the mind, instead of situating the mind, then there would be no eternal consciousness in us. If the brain situates the mind, though, as we have been saying, then the human being is an incarnate spirit and there is an eternal consciousness in us, and there is or can be a journey in time where we go from unconsciousness through partial consciousness to full consciousness.

Now if "we can know more than we can tell," then in the study of brain processes we are studying what we can tell, and in the study of thought processes we are studying what we can know. What we can tell is what we can express in words and music. What we can know overlaps with what we can tell but goes beyond it on account of our indwelling in the particulars of what we know, my indwelling in what Shakespeare calls "the particulars of my life."[19] Indwelling corresponds to being situated. There is the indwelling of the mind in the brain, of the soul in the body, and it is out of this indwelling that we can know more than we can tell.

Yet is dwelling in "the particulars of my life" the same as dwelling in my body or dwelling in my brain? Consider again the hemispheres of the brain, the realm of words and the realm of music, but consider now the process of composition. I think of a friend who was a band director and attended a workshop on composing led by a jazz composer who said "You have to be at peace to compose." To be at peace is to dwell peacefully in your brain and in your body. That peaceful indwelling makes it possible to compose words and music. Or again I could say to be at peace is to dwell peacefully in "the particulars of my life," and that peaceful indwelling makes it possible for me to compose. To compose I have to be composed.

Dwelling in the particulars seems to have been the method of the Renaissance. It is what Paul Valery called "the method of Leonardo da Vinci,"[20] or that is how I interpret Leonardo's motto *ostinato rigore*, "obstinate rigor," as if he were never satisfied with a tacit knowing of particulars. Leaving behind him many incomplete works, Leonardo asked himself again and again in his notebooks, "Tell me if anything has ever been accomplished" (*Di mi se mai fa fatta alcuna cosa*).[21] Never to be satisfied with a tacit knowing of particulars makes for great difficulty in finishing. I can know more than I can tell in telling the story, but if I try always to tell all I can know, the story will always be unfinished.

It seems the mind and the brain are related in just this way: the mind is to the brain as what we can know to what we can tell. "Technically, every work of art comes into being in the same way as the cosmos—by means of catastrophes," Kandinsky says, "which ultimately create out of the cacophony of the various instruments that symphony we call the music of the spheres."[22] Something similar could be said from the viewpoint of an information theorist like Michel Serres, for whom the main concepts are *information* and *noise,* and the creative process, the *genesis,* as Serres calls it,[23] is the emergence of information or of the message from the background noise, like a message in a bottle coming out of the thundering surf of the sea. We can know more than we can tell insofar as we can know the noise in the background as well as the message in the foreground.

This knowing of the mind that comes of indwelling in the particulars of our life is like standing on the seashore and listening to the thunder of the surf, while our telling our story to one another is like trying to make ourselves heard above the thunder of the surf. "We listen to our inmost selves," Martin Buber says, "—and do not know which sea we hear murmuring."[24] We listen to the murmuring, or to the thunder of the surf, or then again, to use an equal and opposite metaphor, we listen to the silence, as "we all have within us a center of stillness surrounded by silence."

"If we had a keen vision and feeling of all ordinary human life," George Eliot says in *Middlemarch,* "it would be like hearing the grass grow or the squirrel's heart beat, and we should die of that roar which lies on the other side of silence."[25] If the brain situates the mind, it situates the words and the music, it situates what we can express in words and in music ("All art constantly aspires towards the condition of music," Walter Pater says).[26] The mind, while finding expression in words and music is aware also of the inexpressible, the surrounding silence, the "roar which lies on the other side of silence." "There is indeed the inexpressible," Wittgenstein says. "This *shows* itself; it is the mystical."[27]

Does the Body Situate the Soul?

If the brain situates the mind, it does so by situating the basic expressions of the mind such as words and music. So too if the body situates the soul, it does so insofar as the body is the expression of the soul. We could say *the human body is the poem of the Renaissance*, thinking of Michelangelo and Leonardo da Vinci. It is the poem of the Renaissance insofar as the body is the expression of the soul. "A good painter has two chief objects to paint, man and the intention of his soul," Leonardo says. "The former is easy, the latter hard because he has to represent it by the attitude and movement of the limbs," and again, "A figure is not praiseworthy if there does not appear in it the action that expresses the feeling of the spirit."[28]

Magic and science and religion all come together in the Renaissance, it seems, science having to do with the human body in relation to the body of the world, magic with the human soul in relation to the soul of the world, and religion with the body in relation to the soul. Thus the art of the Renaissance is largely religious. In spite of these differences of category, it seems, the Renaissance was one thing. "When Petrarca, age 22, in the Church of Santa Chiara at Avignon on April 6th, 1327, caught sight of a lovely girl, his heart pounded or stopped or leapt into his throat," James Hillman says in his lecture on "The Thought of the Heart." "His soul had been assailed by beauty. Was this when the Renaissance began?"[29]

Nowadays these categories are much more separate from one another, magic and science and religion, and yet we could still speak of the human body in relation to the body of the world and of the body in relation to the soul. But if we were to speak of the human soul in relation to the soul of the world, as W. B. Yeats did, it might sound as if we were dabbling in the occult. T. S. Eliot wrote a critique of that in his essay *After Strange Gods*.[30] If we speak though of the body in relation to the soul, we are coming back to the concept of the human body as an expression of the human soul. "The human body is the best picture of the human soul," Wittgenstein says in his *Philosophical Investigations*,[31] but does he mean what Leonardo meant when he spoke of the painter representing "the intention of the soul" by "the attitude and movement of the limbs" and in "the action that expresses the feeling of the spirit"?

I'm ready to go with the Renaissance on all of these things, the human body in relation to the body of the world, the human soul in relation to the soul of the world, and the body in relation to the soul. Let us consider these relations.

Speaking of the body of the world, we can say the curvature of space is due to matter, according to the general theory of relativity. I want to infer from this that matter is a dimension, a fifth dimension if space is three-dimensional and time is a fourth dimension; for if the curvature of space is due to matter, if for example light rays bend in the vicinity of large masses like the sun, then matter *situates* as well as *being situated*. The relation of the human body to the body of the world, if this is so, is one of measurement in terms of these dimensions. I don't mean to say the universe is on a human scale, far from it, but only to say that our measurements are human, even when what we are measuring is far beyond us in its dimensions. I think of the architect Le Corbusier and his idea of "the modulor" (*le modulor*) which he describes as "a harmonious measure to the human scale, universally applicable to architecture and mechanics."[32] His "modulor" is a six-foot-tall human being with his arm raised, used as a unit of measure in building.

An equal and opposite situation exists on the small scale, the quantum scale, where we are measuring things that are far below the human scale, such as particle trajectories. Here again

I want to think of matter as a dimension, and here I would en-vision the matter coordinate as the DeBroglie wave length of an elementary particle, such as an electron or a proton, a wave *length* to be coordinate with the space and time coordinates. So matter as a dimension would be the curvature of space on the large scale and the wave length of an elementary particle on the small scale. The large is larger than human, and the small is smaller than human in scale, and yet both are measured in human measurements.

Matter as a dimension on the human scale itself is the human brain as situating the mind, the human body as situating the soul. How do we come down from the curvature of space to the human body and the human brain, or how do we come up from the wave length of an elementary particle to the human brain and the human body? There is the *equivalence prin-ciple* in general relativity to bring us down from gravitational masses to inertial masses, and there is the *correspondence prin-ciple* in quantum theory to bring us up from wave lengths on the quantum level to classical wave lengths. Equivalence and correspondence, I gather, are principles for relating the large and the small to the human scale.

There is then "a harmonious measure to the human scale, universally applicable to architecture and mechanics," as Le Corbusier says, and it is the human body. Thus I want to in-terpret our science as having to do with the human body in re-lation to the body of the world. Yet "All we know," as William Harvey says in the dedication of his treatise on the circulation of the blood, "is still infinitely less than all that still remains unknown."[33] Is the realm of the unknown that of the soul?

If we make a distinction between *problem* and *mystery*, like Gabriel Marcel, then the realm of the unknown as problem be-longs to science, and the realm of the unknown as mystery is that of the soul. "That which shows itself and at the same time withdraws is the essential trait of what we call the mystery," Heidegger says.[34] Showing and withdrawing is the essential trait of mystery and, we could say, of the soul itself. It is a trait that appears in the paradoxes of the Gospel, "He who finds his life will lose it, and he who loses his life for my sake will find it" (Matthew 10:39). Here the Greek word *psyche* translated as "life" is literally "soul." The paradox, I believe, is that of willingness and hope, willingness to die and yet hope to live. Thus if I am unwilling to die, I will die anyway, "He who finds his life will lose it," but if I am willing to die and yet hope to live, I will find life, "he who loses his life for my sake will find it."

Translating *psyche* as "life," though its literal meaning is "soul," gives us the meaning of soul, how it is a matter of life and death. Taking it to be "mystery," moreover, "that which shows itself and at the same time withdraws," tells us life shows itself and at the same time withdraws in death, as if to say it withdraws but does not cease to exist in death. There is a problem of death and a mystery of death. The problem, I think, is "If I must die someday, what can I do to fulfil my desire to live?" The mystery that shows and withdraws in death is that of eternal life. Thus I wrote in my first book, *The City of the Gods*, "Eternal life, rather than being a soluble but unsolved problem, would be an inexhaustible source of soluble problems."[35] That inexhaustible source then is what I am calling "mystery."

"I call the comportment which enables us to keep open to the meaning hidden in technology, *openness to the mystery*," Heidegger says, after defining mystery as "that which shows itself and at the same time withdraws." He is thinking then of mystery as "the meaning hidden in technology." I am thinking rather of the meaning hidden in life and death, the mystery of eternal life, but we could also speak here of an openness to the mystery. "Releasement toward things" (*Gelassenheit*) and "openness to the mystery" is a comportment toward the meaning hidden in technology but even more toward the meaning hidden in life and death.

Letting be or "releasement toward things" (*Gelassenheit*) and "openness to the mystery" make sense if we make a distinction between the things of life entering and passing and our relation to the things. Letting be and openness to the mystery are relations to the things. Another example would be the Serenity Prayer, "O God, give me the serenity to accept the things I cannot change, the courage to change the things I can, and the wisdom to know the difference." The "things I cannot change" and "the things I can" are things of life; the serenity, the courage, the wisdom are relations to the things. Making this distinction, therefore, between the things and the relations, we can see our mortality in the things entering and passing, in the realization that all things must pass, but we can see intimations of immortality in our relations to the things.

If then the body situates the soul, the things of life situate our relations to the things. The things of life are like a sequence of scenes in a play, a sequence of situations. So of course the situations situate, but what do they situate? The life of the spirit, I suppose, that is the life of relations, hope and peace and friends and intelligence. Or then again the situations situate like a sequence of scenes in a play and they situate the persons, the *dramatis personae*, the cast of characters. But that is the same as situating the life of the spirit, the life of relations, insofar as the persons are constituted by the life of relations, the *I and thou*, or the *I and it* and the *I and thou*. But does this mean the body situates? Perhaps in dance. And situates the soul? Yes, if we are thinking like Kleist of *the path taken by the soul of the dancer.*

If we speak of "grace" as the illumining of the mind and the kindling of the heart, we can see grace as leading us along the path. If we speak of "grace" as "gracefulness," as Kleist does, then we can say with him "Grace appears most purely in that human form which either has no consciousness or an infinite consciousness."[36] If the body situates the soul, therefore, it does so differently according to the degrees of consciousness, going all the way from "no consciousness" to "an infinite consciousness." All the states of mind in between appear in drama and in the sequence of situations, and the story of these states of mind is "the story of a soul," as Saint Thérèse of Lisieux entitles her autobiography, *Histoire d'une Ame.*[37] There she describes her "little way" of becoming a child to enter the kingdom of God, but she also describes her "trial of faith," her dark night, the dark night of the soul.

Oral storytelling "has nothing to say about states of mind," Padraic Colum says, but "has to be in sentences that can be easily and pleasantly carried over by the human voice."[38] It is the written story thus that is or can be "the story of a soul," but drama too can reenact the soul's story—thus the French film *Thérèse* (1986), directed by Alain Cavalier with Catherine Mouchet playing Saint Thérèse, acts out "the story of a soul," even the dark night, her "trial of faith" where she speaks of "a wall which reaches right up to the heavens," and in the written story she adds, "when I sing of the happiness of heaven and of the eternal possession of God, I feel no joy in this, for I sing simply what I want to believe."[39] In this same period she coughed up blood, but she took this as a joyful sign from the Lord "that my entrance into eternal life was not far off."[40]

In outline, the soul's story begins in the standpoint of the person before others, like that of Saint Augustine as a young teacher of rhetoric, then goes on to the standpoint of the person before self, like that of his *Soliloquies*, and then on to the standpoint of the person before God, like that of his *Confessions*. It is at this point, the person before God, that "the trial of faith" that Saint Thérèse experienced can occur. In his *Dark Night of the Soul* Saint John of the Cross says he is telling "the way and manner which the soul follows upon the road of the union of love with God."[41] That is the road that Saint Thérèse was following, and that was her goal, "the union of love with God."

When I read the words of Saint Thérèse about her "trial of faith," "when I sing of the happiness of heaven and of the eternal possession of God, I feel no joy in this, for I sing simply what I want to believe," I thought of the essay of William James, *The Will to Believe*, written about the same time or just a few years before (1896).[42] I would make a distinction, though, between *will* and *willingness,* and I would say faith in eternal life, like that of Saint Thérèse, is not simply a will to believe in eternal life but is rather a combination of *willingness* and *hope,* a willingness to die and yet a hope to live. It is like the willingness to walk alone and yet the hope to walk un-alone. Faith then is not simply will but willingness and hope, as in Dag Hammarskjöld's words at the turning point of his life, "Thanks!" and "Yes!" There is a "Thanks!" and "Yes!" like this in *The Story of a Soul.*

Body situates soul, therefore, as the things of life situate life, the situations that arise in a life like scenes in a play, and the story of the soul is the story of relating to these things, these situations, acting in these scenes. "Thanks!" and "Yes!" express fundamental relations, "Thanks!" to the past and "Yes!" to the future. "We all have within us a center of still-ness surrounded by silence," Dag Hammarskjöld's words at the beginning of his brochure for the Meditation Room at the UN suggest a centering of the soul in the body. "There is an ancient saying that the sense of a vessel is not in its shell but in the void. So it is with this room," he concludes. "It is for those who come here to fill the void with what they find in their center of stillness."[43]

Body as a vessel of soul thus has its sense not in its shell but in the void. Something like this is true also of the brain as situ-ating the mind insofar as mind or spirit is "pure self-identity within otherness," as Hegel defines it.[44] What he is talking about, I think, is the movement from the standpoint of the person before others to that of the person before self. If we go on from there to the standpoint of the person before God, we find what Meister Eckhart calls the divine desert "where the spark of the soul is more at peace than in itself."[45] So if "it is for those who come here to fill the void with what they find in their center of stillness," it will be filled with the presence of others or the presence of self or the presence of God.

Presence then is what fills the void, "real presences" as George Steiner calls them. If "the sense of a vessel is not in its shell but in the void," space and time and matter as dimen-sions constitute the shell, but presence fills the void. The brain situates the mind, the body situates the soul, and matter generally situates as well as being situated in space and time. I started off saying events were in the dimensions, but now I am saying presences. I suppose that is what an event is, a presence. Instead of "eternal life belongs to those who live in the present," as Wittgenstein says, I want to say *eternal life belongs to those who live in the presence.*

Real Presences

We listen to our inmost selves—and do not know which sea
we hear murmuring.
—Martin Buber

If "we all have within us a center of stillness surrounded by silence," as Dag Hammarskjöld says in his brochure for the Meditation Room at the UN, the surrounding silence can be interpreted as the surrounding presence of God. If I take it that way, my own indwelling in my center is surrounded by the presence of God, and my own indwelling is my presence to myself, and if this is the background of my awareness, there is in the foreground the presence of others.

Going from the presence of others to presence to self to the presence of God describes a spiritual journey like that of Saint Augustine. He goes from the rhetorical standpoint before others as a young teacher of rhetoric, to the meditative standpoint before self in his *Soliloquies*, to the contemplative standpoint before God in his *Confessions*. I take this to be an archetypal pattern of the spiritual journey. I see larger visions of history in this same pattern, Vico's rhetorical vision of *corso* and *ricorso,* Hegel's meditative vision of "the phenomenology of spirit," and Saint Augustine's own contemplative vision of the City of God. Let us consider the spiritual journey that goes from one standpoint to another, from the presence of others, to presence to self, to the presence of God.

There is a rejection of "the metaphysics of presence" in the work of Paul De Man and Jacques Derrida with their method of "deconstruction."[1] What is being rejected, it seems, is the primacy of the spoken word over the written word, as the speaker is *present* whereas the writer can be absent. As for the primacy of the spoken word, I think of a deaf student I once had who told me he thought the deaf were more handicapped than the blind, for the language is primarily a spoken language, thus available to the blind but not to the deaf. Yet the deaf student *told* me that, using the spoken language. Actually there *is* a primacy of the spoken word, I think, but the written word has made an essential difference, the recording of the past. Presence, as I am speaking or writing of it here, though—presence of others, presence to self, presence of God—is relationship, no matter whether it appears in speaking or in writing.

"Real presences," then, as George Steiner calls them,[2] are what I am concerned with. If we make a distinction between conceptual knowledge and relational knowledge, then our knowledge of "real presences" is relational, like Saint Paul saying "I know whom I have believed" (2 Timothy 1:12). Our knowledge of others and of ourselves and of God is primarily relational like this, where our conceptual knowledge comes under "the cloud of unknowing." Saint Augustine's prayer "May I know me!" May I know thee!" find its answer thus in "real presences."

The Presence of Others

Writing from the rhetorical standpoint before others, Newman tells his own story in his *Apologia,* and Vico tells the larger story in his *New Science.* If I write from the standpoint of relational knowing like Saint Paul to the Romans or the Corinthians or the Galatians, I can go beyond the hope of acceptance and the fear of rejection by others, though the hope and the fear are there in my words. I can transcend the hope and the fear with my relational knowing of the people to whom I am speaking or writing. "I know. But . . . I don't understand," says Avremel the entertainer in Elie Wiesel's *Trial of God.* "That's because of your profession," Mendel answers. "All your life you tried to entertain. To make people laugh. To do so, you had to learn to know them—not to understand them."[3] So there is a relational knowing that is just knowing and not understanding, and there is a relational knowing that is understanding.

To know people without understanding them, like an entertainer, is to know what will make them laugh and generally to know how they will respond. To know them with understanding, though, is to *pass over* as I call it, to enter into their feeling and imagining and thinking and resolving, to enter in by a kind of empathy. *Passing over* is never total but is always partial and incomplete. And there is an equal and opposite process of *coming back* to oneself. When Kafka says "Our relation to our fellow men is that of prayer, our relation to ourselves, that of effort; from prayer we draw the strength for effort,"[4] I think he is alluding to the element of mystery, the element of the unknown we find in one another and that always limits our ability to understand one another.

To recognize the mystery in the other, I think, is to enter into an *I and thou* relationship with the other. It is possible then to tell my own story from the standpoint of *I and thou,* as Newman seems to do in his *Apologia,* and it is possible also to tell the larger story from this standpoint, as Vico seems to do in his *New Science.* Telling the story from this standpoint gets us into what Vico calls "poetic wisdom,"[5] for we are dealing with human affairs, the course of human events, where, as Aristotle says, "poetry is something more philosophic and of graver import than history, since its statements are of the nature rather of universals, whereas those of history are singulars."[6]

Poetic wisdom then, as Vico calls it, is the same, I want to say, as relational knowing, and I say to myself "Choose wisdom!" thinking "No fool like an old fool," and meaning by choosing wisdom to choose the life of the spirit, the life of relatedness, the life of hope and peace and friends and intelligence.

"Keep me friendly to myself, keep me gentle in disappointment," the prayer Kathleen Norris comes across in *Dakota*,[7] suggests three concentric circles, an outer circle of our relation with others, hopefully gentle, where disappointment can occur; an inner circle of our relation with ourselves, hopefully friendly, and an innermost circle of our relation with God in prayer. The disappointment that can occur in the outer circle of relation with others arises from our expectations. I think of "the four perturbations of the mind" Saint Augustine mentions in his *Confessions*, desire and gladness and fear and sadness.[8] To speak of them as "perturbations of the mind" implies the ancient ideal of peace of mind. The prayer moves in the same direction, inner peace. Telling the story as Newman does, and even telling the larger story as Vico does, can also move in that direction, toward peace of mind.

Newman describes his own spiritual voyage as a coming home to a peace of mind, a coming into port after a rough sea. "I have been in perfect peace and contentment; I never have had one doubt," he says in the last chapter of his *Apologia*. "I was not conscious to myself, on my conversion, of any change, intellectual or moral, wrought in my mind," and yet he does call it "my conversion." "I was not conscious of firmer faith in the fundamental truths of Revelation, or of more self-command; I had not more fervour; but it was like coming into port after a rough sea; and my happiness on that score remains to this day without interruption."[9] As he describes it, then, conversion means becoming what you are.

There is a coming to peace of mind also in the larger story, as Vico says human beings "at first feel without perceiving, then they perceive with a troubled and agitated spirit, finally they reflect with a clear mind."[10] Newman thus in his childhood, as he describes it, at first feels without perceiving, then as a young man perceives with a troubled and agitated spirit, and then in the end reflects with a clear mind. Newman stays there in that reflection with a clear mind, but there is no staying there for Vico who has it that the cycle is repeated ever and again in the larger story. He finds repose of mind, rather, in the contemplation of "ideal eternal history," the pattern that is repeated ever and again in the *corso* and *ricorso* of history, and it is this pattern realized ever and again that he thinks of as "divine providence." So for him "Wisdom sits outside the spectacle of death's pageants, viewing the dialectic between the two poles of human existence," reason and feeling.[11]

It is the presence of others, nevertheless, that is essential both in the life story and in the larger story told from the rhetorical standpoint. For both are seeking to persuade. Newman in telling his story is in the presence of others, and he even names them in the end, saying "And I earnestly pray for all this whole company, with a hope against hope, that all of us, who once were so united, and so happy in our union, may even now be brought at length, by the Power of the Divine Will, into One Fold and under One Shepherd."[12] Vico too is seeking to persuade, seeking "a self-aware balance between the twin barbarisms of sense and reflection, which arise when we adhere exclusively to one or the other pole of our essential nature," and he seeks to strike the balance with "the lightning stroke of the invincible enthymeme,"[13] the basic rhetorical argument.

"Joy comes softly," as in the ancient Chinese saying,[14] and if we think of the love of God, like Spinoza, as joy at the thought of God, then the persuasive argument of rhetoric has to bring us to joy at the thought. The enthymeme, the rhetorical argument, is usually defined as a syllogism with one of the premises implicit, but "the invincible enthymeme" that Vico speaks of seems to mean something more, a combination of reason and emotion. It is an argument that brings us to joy at the thought. I think of C. S. Lewis and his autobiography, *Surprised by Joy*, and his story of being led by joy eventually to embrace Christian faith, defining joy as "an unsatisfied desire which is itself more desirable than any other satisfaction."[15] I take it that his pursuit of joy is an extended argument leading him to faith, the argument of all his subsequent works.

It is the transcendence of longing that is driving the life story and also the larger story, according to the argument of joy, "an unsatisfied desire which is itself more desirable than any other satisfaction." We are never satisfied, according to this, with anything less than God, with anything less than transcendence itself. All the same, there is joy at the thought of God, joy at the thought of God-with-us. "Everything that exists is situated," Max Jacob's saying, is about existence not about transcendence. It is the transcendence of our longing, the restlessness of our heart until it rests in God, that points to God's transcendence. If we follow the argument of joy, it demonstrates not the existence but the transcendence of God.

Following the argument of joy, we can be led like C. S. Lewis to an initial theism before actually coming to something like Christian believing. I think of Karl Jaspers and what he calls "a philosophical faith." The contents of such a faith, he says, are three:

> God is.
> There is an absolute imperative.
> The world is an ephemeral stage between God and existence.[16]

It is a faith based on the transcendence of longing, it seems, a faith because longing points to God but does not prove the existence of God, because the heart's longing contains "an absolute imperative," because the world therefore is "an ephemeral stage" between God and the human heart.

So the argument of joy does not carry us all the way to Christian believing, but there is still a leap of faith. And when we take the leap of faith, as C. S. Lewis did, we leave the argument of joy behind. "I believe (if the thing were at all worth recording) that the old stab, the old bittersweet, has come to me as often and as sharply since my conversion as at any time of my life whatever," he says at the end of *Surprised by Joy*. "But now I know that the experience, considered as a state of my own mind, had never had the kind of importance I once gave it. It was valuable only as a pointer to something other and outer."[17]

In the standpoint of the person before others the leap of faith can take many guises, as in the pseudonyms of Kierkegaard such as Climacus and Anti-Climacus. Each guise is a *persona*, a role, a person before others. In the person of Climacus he plays the role of someone contemplating the leap of faith but not yet leaping. In the person of Anti-Climacus he plays the role of someone actually making the leap. Climacus sees faith as living in uncertainty without despairing, but Anti-Climacus sees faith as relating to oneself and willing to be oneself and being grounded transparently in God. Before the leap is taken faith looks like a conscious and willing living in uncertainty, that is, but after the leap it looks like a transparent grounding in God. So the leap is essentially a passage from living in uncertainty to being transparently grounded.

"One who sets out for God does not reach God," Al-Alawi says, "but one who leans upon God for support is not unaware of God."[18] One who is seeking God like Climacus does not reach God, but one who leans upon God for support like Anti-Climacus is not unaware of God. Leaning is believing, I take it, relying on God for support. When you are setting out or seeking, you experience the transcendence of longing, the restlessness of the heart not yet resting in God. When you are leaning upon God for support, you experience resting in God, you experience not just your own believing, your leaning, but also the support. That is what it means, I gather, to be transparently grounded in God.

There is a gap, nevertheless, between the person before others and the person before self, and also between the person before others and the person before God. The Socratic gap, let us call it, thinking of the role of Socrates in Kierkegaard's *Philosophical Fragments*, is the one between the person before others and the person before self. The Kierkegaardian gap proper then, the one Kierkegaard is focusing on in the *Fragments*, is the one between the person before others and the person before God. Faith, as he is conceiving it, is the relationship in which he is living before God, and so it can only be indirectly communicated in his stance before others. It is because of the gap that there is a leap.

"If you ask me to play myself, I will not know what to do," the actor Peter Sellers said. "I do not know who or what I am."[19] That is the Socratic gap, the gap between the person before others and the Delphic "Know thyself!" Even Goethe said in conversation with Eckermann, "I do not know myself, and God forbid that I should."[20] It is possible to tell your life story from the standpoint before others, as Newman does in his *Apologia* and Goethe does in *Poetry and Truth in My Life,* and it is even possible to tell the larger story, as Vico does, from the rhetorical standpoint which is essentially the stance before others. To say nevertheless "I do not know myself, and God forbid that I should" reveals something untold in the telling.

To cross the gap then between the person before others and the person before God is indeed a leap of faith. Saint Augustine does that in his *Confessions,* but he seems there also "to answer critics both inside and outside the Catholic community,"[21] and that seems to locate him in the stance before others. All the same, I do believe that his sustained prayer there is genuine and he really is in the stance of the person before God, and he is telling things untold in the stance before others. Crossing the gap between the person before others and the person before God brings him to that repose in God he speaks of in the beginning when he says "our heart is restless until it rests in You." Thus it appears that the standpoint before others is not entirely left behind even in that before self and that before God, at least when the meditations before self and the confessions before God are written down for others to read.

If we begin then with the presence of others, we can go on from there to presence to self and on to the presence of God without losing the presence of others. That is what is happening, I am beginning to believe, in the *Confessions* of Saint Augustine. It has occurred to me to write a musical version of the *Confessions*. What it would have to be is something like the *Symphony of Psalms* of Stravinsky. Instead of the three psalms Stravinsky uses, Psalm 39:12–13, Psalm 40:1–3, and Psalm 150, there are the three that Saint Augustine mainly uses, Psalms 4 and 42 and 139.[22] Or keeping the idea of three movements, the first could be on the young Augustine in the rhetorical stance before others, the second on Augustine in the meditative stance before self in his *Soliloquies* praying "May I know me! May I know thee!" and the third on Augustine in the contemplative stance before God in his *Confessions* praying "Late have I loved thee!"

Going with Kafka's thought, "our relation to our fellow men is that of prayer," I take this to mean recognizing the mystery of the other, and going with Goethe's, "I do not know myself, and God forbid that I should," I take this to mean recognizing the mystery we are to ourselves, "the reality that we ourselves do not know but at best can only live," as Max Frisch says in his novel *I'm Not Stiller.*[23] So it is not just the person before others who is unknown to himself, as when the actor Peter Sellers says, "If you ask me to play myself, I will not know what to do. I do not know who or what I am," but also the person before self and the person before God. We can't leap over our own shadow.

To recognize the mystery, however, is to cross the gap. We can't leap over our own shadow, but we can take the leap of faith, a leap that comes down in the same place. That image of leaping and coming down in the same place suggests that the ground under our feet was there all along but we became conscious of it when we leaped and came down in the same place. The ground under our feet is an image of the ground of our being, of being "grounded transparently"[24] in God, as Kierkegaard says. So by relating to ourselves and willing to be ourselves, as he says, we are grounded transparently in God. By recognizing the mystery we are to ourselves, that is, and willingly accepting the mystery that we are, we are grounded in the mystery of God.

"I'm alive!" the boy exclaims in Ray Bradbury's story *Dandelion Wine.*[25] It is like the *cogito* of Descartes, "I think, therefore I am," or even more like the earlier *cogito* of Saint Augustine, "I know that I live," and later in answer to the question "Suppose you are mistaken?" his reply "If I am mistaken, I exist" (*si fallor, sum*).[26] So even though "I do not know who or what I am," as Peter Sellers said, or "I don't know myself," as Goethe said, still "I know that I live," "I'm alive!" and even "If I am mistaken, I exist." The *cogito ergo sum* means I am present to myself, even if I am a mystery to myself. There is certainty here even in the midst of uncertainty.

As for the mystery we are to ourselves, it can be an enlightening rather than an obfuscating mystery. If I put together knowing that I am with not knowing who or what I am, I am led to something like Augustine's prayer "May I know me! May I know thee!" Telling the story is somehow an answer, as Isak Dinesen says, to the cry of the heart *Who am I?*[27] All the same, if "we can know more than we can tell," there is inevitably something untold in telling the story, and we can know or at least know our unknowing in this. It seems then in telling the story and in realizing "we can know more than we can tell" we are getting closer and closer to an answer to "May I know me! May I know thee!" and the answer, as we have seen, seems to lie in our relationship with God.

Experience and perception, that is the important distinction to be made here. Experience is consciousness of the subject; perception is consciousness of the object. I learned this distinction from my teacher Bernard Lonergan when he was talking about the consciousness of Christ.[28] When consciousness is seen only as perception, then the subject, the self, is seen as an illusion, "the fictional self" as Michael Gazzaniga calls it,[29] and the only reality is the object. When consciousness is seen also as experience, then the subject is seen also as real. Presence to self thus is consciousness of the subject, consciousness as experience. "If something happens to you, it is merely an event," Irving Howe says, "but if you ponder it and absorb into your consciousness the full significance of what has happened, it becomes an experience."[30]

"I am" and "I will die" are the two fundamental certainties, but there is the uncertainty in the certainty, the mystery, "the reality that we ourselves do not know but at best can only live." Is this reality, this mystery, that of eternal life? That is the question that Saint Augustine is asking himself in his *Soliloquies.* It is the question of "eternal consciousness" that Kierkegaard raises, "If there were no eternal consciousness in a man . . . what then would life be but despair?"[31]

Concepts without experience are empty, according to Kant, and experience without concepts is blind. There is a concept of eternal life, and there is an experience of eternal life. The concept by itself is empty, the experience by itself is blind, but if we bring the concept and the experience together we have something, we have at least a mystery. Of the concept Wittgenstein says, "If by eternity is understood not endless temporal duration but timelessness, then he lives eternally who lives in the present."[32] The experience, I would say, is that of the life of the spirit, the life of hope and peace and friends and intelligence. The concept without the experience is the empty idea of living in the present. The experience without the concept is that of living the life of the spirit, the life of hope and peace and friends and intelligence. But can this life of the spirit live on through death and survive? If we put together the concept of living in the timeless moment and the experience of the deeper life of the spirit, we come to the thought that eternal life belongs to those who live not simply in the present but in the presence.

Is presence to self enough for eternal life? Or is eternal life to be found rather in the presence of God? That is why Saint Augustine prays in his *Soliloquies,* "May I know me! May I know thee!" In his *Phenomenology of Spirit* Hegel is seeking "absolute knowledge," as he calls it, rather than eternal life. The subtitle of his *Phenomenology* is "The Science of the Experience of Consciousness."[33] So he is talking about the same thing that we are talking about here, presence to self. If we are seeking eternal life, we are trying to determine if presence to self is itself already eternal life, and if we are seeking absolute knowledge, we are trying to determine if presence to self is itself already absolute knowledge. What then is presence to self?

If we are seeking eternal life, we can say presence to self is the inner life, and we can suppose life after death is a continuation of what is now the inner life. "We all have within us a center of stillness surrounded by silence," as Dag Hammarskjöld says in his brochure for the Meditation Room at the UN. Eternal life would mean living in our center of stillness. This is presence to self, but it is not separated from the presence of God if we take the surrounding silence to be the surrounding presence of God. If this is eternal life, and it seems that it is, that "we all have within us a center of stillness surrounded by silence," then Pascal seems right when he says all our troubles stem from our inability to sit quietly in a room.[34]

If you are seeking absolute knowledge, Hegel's dream, or "insight into insight," Bernard Lonergan's ideal, "Thoroughly understand what it is to understand," as Lonergan says, "and not only will you understand the broad lines of all there is to be understood but also you will possess a fixed base, an invariant pattern, opening upon all further developments of understanding."[35] It is like Aristotle's notion of God, "a knowing of knowing." If we make the distinction between experience and perception, however, we can see that presence to self is experience rather than perception, and thus is not yet a knowing of knowing or an insight into insight. If we examine our perception then, we find rather a knowing of our unknowing as the nearest thing we have to a knowing of knowing, as in "the cloud of unknowing in the which a soul is oned with God."

There is, to be sure, another kind of knowing besides conceptual knowing, as we have seen, and that is relational knowing, the knowing that comes of relationship with others, with self, and with God, as in Paul's words, "I know whom I have believed" (2 Timothy 1:12). There is a knowing of this kind in presence to self, as also in the presence of others and the presence of God. Hegel's dream of absolute knowledge is one of conceptual knowing and we awaken from that dream to a knowing of our unknowing. All the same, there is a knowing that comes of presence, a relational knowing, a being in touch with the mystery of others, the mystery of ourselves, the mystery of God. I think of the prayer "Give me a light that I may tread safely into the unknown," and of the answer "Go out into the darkness and put your hand into the hand of God. That shall be to you better than light and safer than a known way."[36]

There is in relation to the mystery, then, the double comportment that Heidegger speaks of, letting be and openness to the mystery. There is letting others be, letting oneself be, letting God be, somewhat in the vein of Meister Eckhart speaking of "wandering joy." "A detached man," he says, "experiences such a joy that no one would be able to tear it away from him. But such a man remains unsettled. He who has let himself be, and who has let God be, lives in a wandering joy, or joy without a cause."[37] Here then the answer to the prayer "May I know me! May I know thee!" is to let oneself be and to let God be. Letting be along with openness to the mystery is a knowing, not indeed a conceptual knowing but a relational knowing of oneself and of God.

By relating to myself and willing to be myself, Kierkegaard says, I am "grounded transparently in God." That relating and that transparent grounding is a relational knowing. At the same time, it is, along with the willing, a solution of the problem of love that Rilke poses in his words "To be loved is to be consumed. To love is to give light with inexhaustible oil. To be loved is to pass away. To love is to endure."[38] The problem of being loved arises, it seems, from the lack of self-acceptance, of not willing to be oneself. A person can be very comfortable with loving, for instance with loving children, but very uncomfortable with being loved, and can be inclined always to withdraw from others who show love. By relating to myself and willing to be myself I am able to let myself be loved instead of always shying away from love.

Eternal life would be an eternal presence to self, but it is conceivable only if it opens upon the presence of others and the presence of God. I think of Henry Vaughan's lines,

> I saw Eternity the other night,
> Like a great ring of pure and endless light,
> All calm, as it was bright

suggesting the great circle of life and light and love, that is "from God and of God and towards God," and of his lines,

> They are all gone into the world of light,
> And I alone sit lingering here

suggesting the presence of the others who belong to his life.[39]

If eternal life is in the great circle of life and light and love, and presence to self mediates between the presence of others and the presence of God, then presence to self is not the same as autonomy or self-sufficiency, but spirit is relatedness and the life of spirit is the life of relatedness, the life of hope and peace and friends and intelligence. "So, waiting, I have won from you the end: God's presence in each element," the words of Goethe that Martin Buber quotes as epigraph to *I and Thou*,[40] suggest the presence of others and the presence of God with presence to self coming between them. For me the comprehensive formula is that of the Gospel of John, *I in them and thou in me* (John 17:23), real presences but indwelling, following Christ, making his Father my Father, making his God my God.

Presence to self, therefore, meaning "we all have within us a center of stillness surrounded by silence," suggests a life of living toward eternal life instead of simply living toward death. The journey toward eternal life would mean living in the quiet eye of a moving storm. I think of *Rejoice in the Lamb* by the insane poet Christopher Smart, set to music by Benjamin Britten. "Hallelujah from the heart of God," he sings,

For God the Father Almighty plays upon a harp
Of stupendous magnitude and melody . . .
For at that time malignity ceases
And the devils themselves are at peace . . .
For this time is perceptible to man
By a remarkable stillness and serenity of soul.[41]

The poet's madness is the moving storm, but there is the quiet eye where there is "a remarkable stillness and serenity of soul."

It is a moving eye of a moving storm, and so I have to keep moving to stay in my center of stillness. Thus "the future—any future—was simply one step at a time out of the heart," as Patricia McKillip says in one of her stories.[42] The heart is that center of stillness where thought and feeling meet, where both thought and feeling are honored, and where they join together in an alliance, and the one step at a time is one situation at a time, as it arises, seen and judged and acted upon from the vantage point of that center of stillness surrounded by silence. So I move with the moving eye of the moving storm by taking one step at a time out of the heart.

To believe in eternal life is to rely on "eternal consciousness," as Kierkegaard calls it in *Fear and Trembling,* "grounded transparently in God," as he says in *Sickness unto Death.*[43] "Eternal consciousness" is presence to self, "grounded transparently in God" is presence of God. It is indeed a leap of faith to believe in eternal life. I think of the cry of the man in the Gospel of Mark, "Lord, I believe: help thou mine unbelief!"(Mark 9:4). It is again the prayer of the *Soliloquies,* "May I know me! May I know thee!" as if to say knowing me is inseparable from knowing thee, eternal consciousness is inseparable from being grounded transparently in God. If I say "Lord, I believe: help thou mine unbelief!" I am in an *I and thou* relationship with God where who I am is inseparable from who God is.

If the story alone can answer the cry of the heart *Who am I?* as Isak Dinesen says, the life story is encompassed in the larger story of God. As I understand it, the larger story is of all coming from God and all returning to God. The mystery then remains of who I am and who God is, penetrated not by conceptual knowing but only by relational knowing. If I follow Christ, making his God my God, I enter into a personal relationship with the Absolute, and what insight I have into the cry of the heart arises from my sense of being on a journey with God in time. It is an unfinished journey, like an incomplete sentence.

"God does not play dice" (*Gott wurfelt nicht*), Einstein's dictum, criticizing the statistical interpretation of the quantum theory, suggests an interpretation of the larger story and of the life story along the lines of Spinoza's thinking. I want to suggest instead an interpretation arising out of "God is spirit," the saying of Jesus to the woman at the well (John 4:24). It differs from Spinoza's conception of God's two attributes, thought and extension. "God is spirit" excludes the idea of extension as an attribute. What I understand by "God is spirit" is that God acts spiritually, kindling hearts and illumining minds. A journey with God then is a spiritual journey. So even if my journey with God is an unfinished journey, with an unfinished meaning like an incomplete sentence, it is nevertheless a spiritual journey with God who is spirit and has in it the hope of eternal life.

Thinking of Einstein, I think also of his sense of being on an unfinished journey, even at the end of his life, having failed to acheive his ideal of a unified field theory. "However that may be," he says, referring to those who disagree with him on the quantum problem, "Lessing's comforting word stays with us: the aspiration to truth is more precious than its assured possession."[44] Kierkegaard too, arguing against Hegel's claim to absolute knowledge, says "Lessing has said that, if God held all truth in His right hand, and in His left the lifelong pursuit of it, he would choose the left hand."[45] It does indeed seem that presence to self culminates not in all truth, or absolute knowledge, but in the lifelong pursuit of truth, and so the journey of life is always an unfinished journey, a journey toward eternal life.

If God holds the lifelong pursuit of truth in his left hand and I choose the left hand, my life becomes a quest of wisdom. I think of Saint Augustine's quest of wisdom that he describes in his *Confessions*. In fact, I keep telling myself "Choose wisdom!" in this my later life, thinking "No fool like an old fool." Choosing the left hand of God, I am like Rilke in his *Stories of God*, welcoming the Stranger whom he suspects is the left hand of God. "Do you still remember God?" he asks, and the Stranger, whose eyes seem to reflect long avenues going back to "a distant shimmering point," replies after a long pause, "Yes, I still remember God."[46] I have to ask myself that same question, "Do you still remember God?" and let it take me on those avenues of memory to that distant shimmering point to see if I too can say "Yes, I still remember God."

The Presence of God

A search for God in time and memory is something I have been conducting since my second book, actually entitled *A Search for God in Time and Memory* (1969).[47] Now, though, I am reading Erik Kandel, *In Search of Memory* (2006), subtitled "The Emergence of a New Science of Mind," an autobiography and a history of a new biology of mind by a Nobel Prize winner.[48] Going with the idea presented above in the second chapter that matter is a dimension and that the brain situates the mind, I am interpreting Kandel's work as having to do with the brain situating memory. The idea of situating memory is something we find in Renaissance memory theatres and memory palaces, as they were called, and in the ancient rhetorical art of memory. The modern search for memory, I take it, is an effort to situate memory in the human brain with scientific precision.

To remember God, like *dikhr Allah* in Islam, can mean to keep God in mind, to practice the presence of God. It is a focus of attention, along the lines of Malebranche's saying, "Attention is the natural prayer of the soul."[49] I came across that idea in Walter Benjamin speaking of Kafka and saying "Even if Kafka did not pray—and this we do not know—he still possessed in the highest degree what Malebranche called 'the natural prayer of the soul': attentiveness. And in this attentiveness he included all living creatures, as saints include them in their prayers," and I found it also in Paul Celan speaking of attention in poetry and saying "The attention which the poem pays to all that it encounters . . ." is "a kind of concentration mindful of all our dates."[50] The attention widens in Benjamin to include "all living creatures" and in Celan to include "all our dates," and yet both say with Malebranche that it is "the natural prayer of the soul."

Studying attention from the viewpoint of brain science, Eric Kandel speaks of the spatial map that we each have inside our minds.[51] It occurs to me that there may be a time map as well with "all our dates." As Newton saw space and time as the divine sensorium, Kant saw them instead as the human sensorium, and present-day brain science can investigate them as the human sensorium. Without going back to Newton's idea of the divine sensorium, we can still see our attention as "the natural prayer of the soul" if we include "all living creatures" and ask a question like that of Leibniz, "Why is there anything at all and not rather nothing?"[52] Attention is selective—we pay attention to some things and not to others. It becomes "the natural prayer of the soul," it seems, when it becomes inclusive of "all our dates" and "all living creatures."

"Why is there anything at all and not rather nothing?" the wonder of existence, leads to the insight that God exists. If we no longer take for granted what is most taken for granted, the existence of things, then attention does become "the natural prayer of the soul." Let us consider what happens to attention as prayer if we include "all our dates" and "all living creatures."

If we include "all our dates," attention as prayer becomes what it is in the *Confessions* of Saint Augustine. There is his life story and there is the larger story of the genesis of the world and there is the link between the two in his meditation on time and memory. The life story and the larger story I find also in the autobiography of Geronimo, for instance, prefacing his life story with the Apache story of creation.[53] Turning the life story and the larger story into prayer, however, along with their link in time and memory, Saint Augustine exclaims "Late have I loved you, beauty so old and so new, late have I loved you!"[54] seeing time up against eternity—time: "late have I loved you" and eternity: "beauty so old and so new"—time as a changing image of eternity, time, as it were, catching up to eternity.

"Late have I loved you, beauty so old and so new, late have I loved you!" means the connection of time and eternity is *I and thou*. Reading Saint Augustine's meditation on time and memory, Martin Heidegger asks the question "Am I my time?" and wants to answer "Yes." What I see in the meditation is a relationship of *I and thou* between time and eternity, and so I would want to say instead "No, I am *in* my time," in order to leave the door open to eternal life.[55] "Eternal consciousness," as Kierkegaard calls it, would be the consciousness of the human *I* in relationship with the divine *thou*. It would be the consciousness of the heart that is restless until it rests in God.

As I cannot leap over my own shadow, so the mystery I am to myself is inseparable from the mystery God is to me. Thinking back to my beginning, as Saint Augustine does in his *Confessions*, brings me back through consecutive memories to scattered recollections, and to go on from there as he does to nothingness in the beginning can seem more belief than memory. What I am really meeting *at the edge of memory* is my own mystery and the mystery of God. Thinking back, therefore, *andenken* as Heidegger calls it, is ultimately thinking back to mystery. I am in the mystery that appears in the parable of the sparrow's flight, the parable proposed to King Edwin of Northumbria by his wise counselor, how our life is like a sparrow's flight through a warm and lighted hall, coming in from darkness outside and going again into darkness.[56]

So if we know no more of life and death than the Northumbrians, still we can call that darkness "mystery," the mystery before and after life, and we can enter like Jesus himself into a personal relation with the mystery of God. That is what Saint Augustine seems to come to in his *Confessions,* a personal knowledge, a relational knowledge, that is, of himself and of God, answering his prayer "May I know me! May I know thee!" Trying to reenact that knowledge for myself, I think again of those words of Dag Hammarskjöld, "We all have within us a center of stillness surrounded by silence." The center of stillness is the answer to "May I know me!" and the surrounding silence is the answer to "May I know thee!"

If now I include "all living creatures" in the scope of attention, the very personal starting point, "I am," has to be enlarged to "I am alive." I think of the moment in Ray Bradbury's story *Dandelion Wine* when the boy who is the main character says "I'm alive!" in the middle of wrestling with his brother. His brother says "Are you alright?" but the boy gives a great soundless shout inside of himself, "I'm alive! I'm really alive!"[57] Saint Augustine too has an anticipation of the *cogito* of Descartes not only in the form of "I am" but also in the form of "I am alive." If we begin with *I am* we come to Being, but if we begin with *I'm alive* we come to "all living creatures." I think of the verses by Cecil Alexander,

> All things bright and beautiful,
> All creatures great and small,
> All things wise and wonderful,
> The Lord God made them all.

and of the books by the veterinarian James Herriot named after each of these verses.[58]

There are really two starting points in the *cogito* of Descartes: "I think" and "I am," thought and existence. If we add "I am alive," we have three, and the one we have added, "I am alive," mediates between thought and existence. "I know that I live" is Saint Augustine's formulation of "I am alive" in his essay *On the Trinity* and is meant as an answer to skepticism like his later formula in *The City of God,* "If I am mistaken, still I am."[59] Those words "I know that I live" seem to echo the words "I know that my redeemer liveth" (Job 19:25), the words sung many centuries later in Handel's *Messiah,* and "I know that I live" probably means the life of the spirit, the life of hope and peace and friends and intelligence, the eternal life that can live on through death.

"I know that I live" and "I know that my redeemer lives" go together in a faith that is at once a willingness to die and yet a hope to live. The knowing here is "personal knowledge" as Michael Polanyi calls it. "We can know more than we can tell," his principle, we have resolved into telling the story and knowing the relationship. "I know that I live" resolves then into telling my story and knowing the relationship that is my self ("a relation that relates to itself" as Kierkegaard says).[60] "I know that my redeemer lives" resolves in the same way into telling the story of my redeemer and knowing the relationship with "my Father and your Father, my God and your God" (John 20:17).

"What is life?" the question posed by the physicist Erwin Schrodinger gave rise to molecular biology.[61] His wave equation is central to quantum mechanics and won him the Nobel Prize in physics. I wrote to him when I was a young man to ask him about the question I posed above in chapter 2, "Is matter a dimension?" and he wrote back a one sentence reply, "Matter is *not* a dimension"! All the same, it may be that matter as a dimension is a fundamental clue to the question "What is life?" If matter *situates,* as well as being situated in space and time, the life that is situated by matter is not itself matter. It may be, as James D. Watson says, "The human genetic script that we are now finalizing will be regarded as the most important book ever to be read."[62] And yet it may be that the human genetic script only *situates* what is more important, the human spirit.

If we take the standpoint of evolution and molecular biology, what are we to say of the presence of God? I think of the collection of essays *Evolution and Molecular Biology* (1998) with the subtitle "Scientific Perspectives on Divine Action."[63] I am inclined, though, to look for divine action in the realm of the spirit rather than in the realm of the uncertainty principle in physics. God is at work, I want to say, not so much in what is happening as in our relation to what is happening. It is as if we were still in the sixth day of creation where God is busy creating human beings. It takes a whole lifetime to create a human being. "God is spirit" (John 4:24) then, and acts spiritually, kindling hearts and illumining minds, and that is how God is at work in the evolution of human beings.

Our own participation in divine action, accordingly, is to "rekindle hearts in a world that grows chill," as Tolkien says, speaking of the role of Gandalf in Middle Earth.[64] Our role is similar to his, it seems, and ours is indeed "a world that grows chill," as in the saying Nietzsche repeats, "God is dead," or in the question that is posed in the Gospel of Luke, "when the Son of man comes, will he find faith on the earth?" (Luke 18:8). The kindling of the heart and the illumining of the mind have to do, it seems, especially with faith, and the world growing chill has to do with the loss of faith. To rekindle hearts is to rekindle the willingness and the hope that constitute faith. To illumine minds is to illumine the way that comes to light in that willingness and hope. Teaching does this from the outside, as Saint Augustine says in his essay *On the Teacher,* while God does it from the inside, working in minds and hearts.

Kant's three questions "What can I know? What should I do? What may I hope?"[65] all converge on this process of kindling hearts and illumining minds. "What can I know?" finds an initial answer in Polanyi's principle, "we can know more than we can tell," but if we consider it further, we come upon something that my sister Carrin pointed out to me, that we oftentimes think we are in one story when actually we are in another. Her prime example was Saint Benedict Joseph Labre, who thought he was in the story of a monk and went from one monastery to another until he ultimately realized he was not in the story of a monk but in that of a pilgrim. To realize we are in a story other than the one we thought is to realize "we can know more than we can tell" in a new way. It is to know the relationship we are living transcends the story we thought we were living.

"What should I do?" then finds its answer in living the relationship, I would say in living the "unconditional relation," as Martin Buber calls it in *I and Thou,* speaking of the *I and thou* of Jesus with his God. "For it is the *I* of unconditional relation in which the man calls his *thou* Father in such a way that he himself is simply Son and nothing else but Son," he says, and "every man can say *thou* and is then *I,* every man can say Father and is then Son."[66] I take it this means making the God of Jesus my God, entering into his relationship with the God he calls Abba, as he says to Mary Magdalene, "my Father and your Father, my God and your God" (John 20:17).

"What may I hope?" then finds its answer in "God-with-us" (Matthew 1:23) as we journey into the unknown, as in the prayer "Give me a light that I may tread safely into the unknown" and the answer "Go out into the darkness and put your hand into the hand of God. That shall be to you better than light and safer than a known way!"[67] We do journey into the unknown, into the darkness, but if we put our hand into the hand of God, then we journey with God. There is hope in that, even the unhoped-for, as in the saying of Heraclitus, "If one does not hope, one will not find the unhoped-for, since there is no trail leading to it and no path."[68] Putting my hand into the hand of God, I walk with God on the way to the unhoped-for.

Espoir and *esperance,* the distinction Jean Giono makes between a hope that is set upon a certain object and a hopefulness that is open to the unhoped-for,[69] that is the distinction we need to make in answering the last question, "What may I hope?" It is like the distinction between will and willingness, will where the heart is set upon a certain object and willingness where the heart is open to the unknown, open to the mystery. Faith thus is a combination of willingness and hope, but a hope that is open to the unhoped-for.

But what is the unhoped-for? A chance meeting? A life after life? As soon as I name these things, the relation of hope to the unhoped-for becomes clearer. I may hope to meet someone who will change my life and make me a new person.

I may hope the life of the spirit, the deeper life of hope and peace and friends and intelligence, will be able somehow to endure death and survive it. The *someone* and the *somehow,* indicate the unknown and the unhoped-for. In Christian believing the someone and the somehow are one and the same, the person of Jesus Christ in his relationship to God.

Here again we encounter "the cloud of unknowing in the which a soul is oned with God." It is an unknowing and yet in it "a soul is oned with God." Short prayer penetrates the cloud of unknowing, "May I know me! May I know thee!" Love penetrates it, "Late have I loved you, beauty so old and so new: late have I loved you!" So the way to the unhoped-for is "the road of the union of love with God." "There is no trail leading to it and no path," Heraclitus says, meaning no guiding expectation, for it is the unexpected. All the same, there is a way insofar as hope leads to the unhoped-for, willingness and hope, that is, letting be and openness to the mystery.

Words and Music

Song is the leap of mind in the eternal breaking out into sound.
—Saint Thomas Aquinas

"You must love the music, not master it," a Chinese grandmother advised one of my students who was feeling frustrated, trying to play a difficult nocturne by Chopin on the piano. "Music must be treated as all things that are eternal, such as love and understanding," she said, "because it is these things that will carry us through the darkness of our lives and the death of our bodies to the moon of everlasting peace."[1]

To place music with "things that are eternal, such as love and understanding" is to say it belongs to the life of the spirit, the life of hope and peace and friends and intelligence. It is like speaking of "the words of eternal life" (John 6:68). Not all words are words of eternal life, and not all music is eternal, but only the words and the music that are expressive of the deeper life, the life of the spirit. There is a connection between words and music, though, when they are expressive of eternal life, as in the definition of song (*canticum*) that Saint Thomas Aquinas gives in his preface to the Psalms, "Song is the leap of mind in the eternal breaking out into sound."[2]

There is a link then between words and music when they are together in song and the song is "the leap of mind in the eternal breaking out into sound." If words and music belong to different hemispheres of the brain, words to the left and music to the right, and the right hand goes with the left hemisphere and the left hand with the right hemisphere, then Kant's problem of the right and left hand which cannot be made to neatly cover one another is also a problem of words and music.[3] A right hand glove, however, can be put on the left hand if it is turned inside out. Similarly we might suppose words are music inside out and music is words inside out. Or at any rate there is a musical inside of words and a verbal inside of music. Does the inside have to do with the eternal, as the inner life becomes the afterlife?

Let me propose that the *theme* is the verbal inside of music and the *inscape* is the musical inside of words. Let us examine these two insides and see if they can help us discover what I call "the music of words," the original unity of words and music, something that will have existed in the beginning if Vico was right that the world's first languages were in song.[4]

Theme: the Verbal Inside of Music

A musical theme, what Wagner called a *leitmotif,* is the verbal inside of a piece of music, we can say, but does it have to do with the eternal? If we say with Plato that time is "a changing image of eternity," then we can say musical themes, not only in sacred music but also in secular music, may have to do with the eternal. Time, and music likewise, can be opaque, can be translucent, can be transparent to eternity. Consider the theme Beethoven used, first in a round and then in the last movement of his last string quartet, with the words,

Grave:	Muss es sein?	Must it be?
Allegro:	Es muss sein!	It must be!
	Es muss sein!	It must be!

In the round the theme is opaque to eternity and has to do with a debt that must be paid, while in the string quartet the theme is translucent or even transparent to eternity and seems to be about going from the *Grave* of infinite resignation ("Must it be?") to the *Allegro* of faith ("It must be! It must be!").[5] So the same melody and the same words can be opaque to eternity in one context and translucent or even transparent to eternity in another.

"Must it be?" the *Grave* of infinite resignation is what we feel here and in the G minor themes of Mozart. That is Kierkegaard's term, "infinite resignation," and he imagines his "knight of infinite resignation" to make the movements of a dancer, "the movements of infinity," as he calls them. "Most people live dejectedly in worldly sorrow and joy; they are the ones who sit along the wall and do not join in the dance," he says. "The knights of infinity are dancers and possess elevation. They make the movements upward, and fall down again; this too is no mean pastime, nor ungraceful to behold. But whenever they fall down they are not able at once to assume the posture, they vacillate an instant, and this vacillation shows that after all they are strangers in the world."[6] But what is infinite resignation? It is the recognition and acceptance of who we are, reluctant maybe but acceptance nonetheless, infinite as a Yes to God's will.

"It must be! It must be!" is the *Allegro* of faith, like "For all that has been—Thanks! To all that shall be—Yes!"as Dag Hammarskjöld exclaims at the turning point of his life. That can seem to be the same as resignation, and yet it is not—the difference is in the joy. In the leap of faith one leaps in the air and comes down in the same place. "But to be able to fall down in such a way that the same second it looks as if one were standing and walking, to transform the leap of life into a walk, absolutely to express the sublime in the pedestrian," Kierkegaard says, "that only the knight of faith can do."[7]

If I speak of the *Grave* of infinite resignation and the *Allegro* of faith, there is nevertheless the "worldly sorrow and joy" of those "who sit along the wall and do not join in the dance," and that too can find musical expression. Saint Augustine speaks of the "four perturbations of the mind": desire and gladness and fear and sadness.[8] In relation to the eternal there is the restlessness of desire, that is the transcendence of longing, there is the joy or gladness of faith, there is the fear or dread that is, however, "a saving experience by means of faith,"[9] and there is the sadness of infinite resignation, "for what I gain by resignation is my eternal consciousness."[10]

Those "four perturbations of the mind" suggest still another and opposite attitude, and that would be peace of mind and heart and soul. I think again of Hammarskjöld's formula, "We all have within us a center of stillness surrounded by silence." Out of the stillness and the silence comes the music, even "the leap of mind in the eternal breaking out into sound." If we can suppose with Vico that the world's first languages were in song, we can imagine the songs expressed desire and gladness and fear and sadness. In his book *The Singing Neanderthals* (2006) Steven Mithen has proposed the hypothesis that the Neanderthals had music but not language.[11] Desire and gladness and fear and sadness, as in our own music, can be expressed in songs without words. So music could have what I am calling a "verbal inside" even in the absence of language.

Or could it? "If we take language as a paradigm, the paradigm is constituted by, first, phonemes, second, words, third, sentences," Levi-Strauss says. "In music you have the equivalent to phonemes and the equivalent to sentences, but you don't have the equivalent to words."[12] Themes are the equivalent to sentences, but if there is really no equivalent to words (what of neums in plainsong?), then themes have to carry all the meaning in music. Wagner thought of musical themes in the *Ring* "not as tags identifying personages, objects, and ideas so much as 'motifs of memory.'"[13] If we think of musical themes generally as *motifs of memory*, then musical themes, like poetry according to Wordsworth, come of "emotion recollected in tranquillity," not simply desire and gladness and fear and sadness then but the recollection of those feelings in tranquillity.

Music and memory then is the relation we must consider to get at theme as the verbal inside of music. A theme is not just perceived but is recognized. So we have to make a distinction between perception and apperception, and take apperception to be recognition, involving memory. Recognition can be far-reaching, going beyond the music. "What we call music in our everyday language is only a miniature," Inayat Khan says, "which our intelligence has grasped from that music or harmony of the whole universe which is working behind everything, and which is the source and origin of nature."[14]

Apperception, as Leibniz conceived it, is the awareness the mind has of itself as it perceives. As Kant conceived it, empirical apperception is consciousness of oneself as a changing phenomenon with a variable content—I think of the Voyage of Life, four paintings by Thomas Cole showing childhood, youth, adulthood, and old age. Pure apperception, according to Kant, is consciousness of the persisting identity of oneself—I think of the *cogito*, "I think therefore I am." Apperception, as I am talking about it here in music, is simply recognition, perception plus memory, but it begins to take on the self-awareness of Leibniz and Kant when one begins to recognize oneself in the music and to join in the music. "Will you, won't you, will you, won't you, will you join the dance?"[15] rather than being one of "the ones who sit along the wall and do not join the dance."

Music as a state of being, therefore, and music as symbolic form is the distinction we are led to as we consider the invitation, "Will you, won't you, will you, won't you, will you join the dance?" I found this distinction in *Jazz Text* by Charles Hartman. "*Music as a state of being*," he says, "as in the day-long or week-long festivals held by Berbers and other tribes, exercises a quite different power over its listeners, *means* in a quite different way, from (in Susanne Langer's phrase) *music as symbolic form*."[16] To join in the music, to join the dance, goes rather with music as a state of being, and if we speak of "the singing Neanderthals" we are speaking, most likely, of music as a state of being. Joining in the music, joining the dance leads to Yeats' question,

> O body swayed to music, O brightening glance,
> How can we know the dancer from the dance?[17]

My own thoughts on this come out in four dances I composed,

Dance of the Winds	*Earth Dance*
O guiding eye,	O mystery that shows
O guarding storm,	and then withdraws,
how can we know	how can we know
the spirit from the wind?	the spirit from the dance?
Fire Dance	*River Dance*
O lonely wish,	O spring of water
impassioned hope,	welling up into eternal life,
how can we know	how can we know
the spirit from the flame?	the spirit from the thirst?[18]

What comes out in these dances is that it is the spirit that is concealed and revealed in the music of the dance. The motifs of memory in Wagner's *Ring* are like these, the wind, the fire, the earth, the water. My question is "How can we know the spirit from the wind, the flame, the dance, the thirst?"

If we go from music as a state of being to music as symbolic form, if we turn for instance to the G-minor works of Mozart, we go from life as a state of being to life as symbolic form. Interpreting my four dances as states of being, we cannot know the spirit from the wind, the flame, the dance, the thirst. Interpreting the four dances as symbolic forms, however, we can know the spirit as "pure self-identity within otherness," as Hegel says,[19] within the otherness of the wind, the flame, the dance, the thirst. In music as a state of being, I am saying, we cannot know the dancer from the dance, but in music as symbolic form we can know the dancer from the dance. This tells us something about "the path taken by the soul of the dancer."[20]

Is it the path of eternal life? Yes, I would say, but in music as a state of being eternal life appears as a state of being, and in music as symbolic form eternal life appears as symbolic form. There is mention of eternal life in my River Dance,

> O spring of water
> welling up into eternal life,
> how can we know
> the spirit from the thirst?

The thirst here is the transcendence of longing, how our heart is restless until it rests in God. As a state of being the thirst is this transcendent longing, and that is eternal life already begun in us. As symbolic form, the thirst is an experience of our capacity for God, *anima est capax Dei*, "the soul is capable of God,"[21] and thus our capacity for eternal life.

"Doubting Thomas," however, is an image in the Gospel of John of the uncertainty surrounding eternal life, an uncertainty the Gospel seeks to resolve with Thomas's profession of faith, "My Lord and my God" (John 20:28). Glenn Most gives a history of the doubt in his *Doubting Thomas* (2006), and believes the doubt has never really been resolved.[22] My own view is that doubt arises always in the quest of certainty—as we try to make sure we become ever more unsure. For me then the solution is to go over from the quest of certainty to the quest of understanding. Doubt is of the essence of the quest of certainty, while faith is of the essence of the quest of understanding. To seek understanding is to let be and be open to the mystery, and that letting be and openness leads to insight.

In music as a state of being we have a guiding and a guarding ("O guiding eye, O guarding storm"), a wish and a hope ("O lonely wish, impassioned hope"), a "mystery that shows and then withdraws," a "spring of water welling up into eternal life." All of this is doubtful in a quest of certainty, and all of this is illuminating in a quest of understanding. If we go over from a quest of certainty to a quest of understanding, we can take these as illuminating, as guiding insights, guiding and guarding, wishful and hopeful, showing and withdrawing, welling up within us. We are acting upon the light we have, taking these as light, as insights, as illuminations. Certainty, on the other hand, is knowing that you know. We are working instead in a knowing unknowing, a "learned ignorance," a "cloud of unknowing in the which a soul is oned with God."

In music as symbolic form we can discern the spirit in the wind, in the flame, in the dance, in the thirst. On the quest of certainty we can't be sure of anything more in this than a symbolic immortality, but in the quest of understanding we can pass over from symbol to reality, from symbolic immortality to the reality of eternal life. Going over then from certainty to understanding, we go over from the symbols to the reality, from the wind that "blows where it will" to the "one that is born of the Spirit" (John 3:8), from the flame to the kindling of the heart, from the dance to the mystery that shows and then withdraws, and from the thirst to the heart's desire.

"Doubting Thomas" is doubting because he is seeking certainty, "Except I shall see in his hands the print of the nails, and put my finger into the print of the nails, and thrust my hand into his side, I will not believe" (John 20:25), but when he sees Jesus he exclaims "My Lord and my God!" (John 20:28), apparently not having put his finger into the print of the nails and thrust his hand into his side, though Jesus invites him to do so. He has gone over from certainty to understanding, though Jesus goes on to say "Thomas, because thou hast seen me, thou has believed: blessed are they that have not seen, and yet have believed"(John 20:29). "Seeing is believing," according to the proverb, but on the quest of understanding "Believing is seeing," we could say, insofar as "faith is seeing light with your heart when all your eyes see is darkness."[23]

"He that lives in hope danceth without musick," George Herbert says,[24] and one who lives in hope can dance also with music, the hope of eternal life I mean, and maybe this is how music comes about and how it ever came about. "The singing Neanderthals," as Steven Mithen calls them, may have had hope of eternal life, for we do know of them that they buried their dead, painting their bodies with red ochre, perhaps as a symbol of life. Music as a state of being, "as in the day-long or week-long festivals held by Berbers and other tribes," has an endlessness about it that does suggest eternal life. Music as symbolic form, on the other hand, has a sense of time as "a changing image of eternity" that also suggests eternal life. "The mystery of music," as Mithen calls it, is the mystery of its origin, as he conceives it, but even more the mystery of its meaning.

Our quest of understanding, when it comes to music, is a search for God in time and memory. Consider again the definition of song Saint Thomas Aquinas gives in his preface to the Psalms, "Song is the leap of mind in the eternal breaking out into sound." Searching for God in time and memory, I find God in memory in the leap of mind, I find God in time in the eternal breaking out into sound. I think of the four memories that Yeats speaks of in *A Vision:* the memory of the events of life, the memory of past lives, the memory of ideas, and the memory of moments of exaltation.[25] "The leap of mind" (*exultatio mentis*) seems to correspond to this last memory, the memory of moments of exaltation. "In the eternal" (*de aeternis habita*) "breaking out into sound" (*prorumpens in vocem*) seems to correspond to what the Chinese grandmother said, "Music must be treated as all things that are eternal, such as love and understanding, because it is these things that will carry us through the darkness of our lives and the death of our bodies to the moon of everlasting peace."

Searching for God then in time and memory, like Saint Augustine in the later parts of his *Confessions,* I come to the question Heidegger finds there, "Am I my time?"[26] If I am my time, I am my story and my song, but if instead I am *in* my time, then I am *in* my story and my song. Being *in* my time leaves the door open to eternal life, whereas being my time seems to close the door with death. "I feel as if I was *inside* a song, if you take my meaning," Sam says in Tolkien's trilogy,[27] and if there is a "verbal inside of music," as we are saying here, there is meaning to being "inside a song."

"How can we know the dancer from the dance?" points to this question, "Am I my time or am I *in* my time?" My interpretation is that the dancer is the human spirit, and the question is how can we know the spirit from the wind, the flame, the dance, the thirst? In music as a state of being we do not yet know the dancer from the dance, I think, because the dancer is not yet differentiated from the dance, and the person is not yet differentiated from the life, but in music as symbolic form we can know, as the dancer is differentiated from the dance, and the person is differentiated from the life, and there we come to a sense of being "inside a song" or inside the song and dance of life. And that leads us on into the musical inside of words, the inscape or inner landscape.

Inscape: the Musical Inside of Words

Inscape, as Gerard Manley Hopkins calls it, is the musical inside of words. "Poetry is in fact speech only employed to carry the inscape of speech for the inscape's sake," he says, "—and therefore the inscape must be dwelt on."[28] Inscape is usually defined as the inwardness or thisness (haecceity) of things as perceived by the poet. If it is essential to poetry, as Hopkins says, it is not surprising that it should be connected with music, as the ancient term *musica,* for instance Saint Augustine's essay *De Musica,* seems to have meant verse set to music. If I say it is the musical inside of words, as the musical theme is the verbal inside of music, I am implying a connection of inscape and musical theme. Consider again the four dances I composed as variations on a theme of Yeats. *Once* may be enough for the inscape, Hopkins says, but *oftening, over-and-overing, aftering* (his italics) may be required.[29]

Now the spirit is the inscape in these four dances, and the question arises again, for the musical inside as for the verbal inside, does it have to do with the eternal? If we think of spirit with Hegel as "pure self-identity within otherness," we are thinking of it in terms of presence to self and the presence of others, but if we think of spirit with the Gospel of John, "God is spirit" (John 4:24), then we are thinking of it in terms of the presence of God. If "real presences" are the eternal in us, then spirit is the eternal. "Man is spirit. But what is spirit? Spirit is the self. But what is the self? The self is a relation which relates itself to its own self," Kierkegaard says,[30] and if he is right, spirit is inwardness and it is the thisness (haecceity) of a person, and so it is the inscape of the human being.

Once and *oftening* and *over-and-overing* and *aftering* of inscape, I think, is what is called recursion, and recursion belongs to music as well as language. Thus Hopkins says "poetry is speech which afters and oftens its inscape." "But is all verse poetry?" he asks. Only when it is *mousike*, he answers, using the ancient Greek term for music.[31] Spirit is the inscape and the recursive element in my four dances, though it is not mentioned in the theme from Yeats. Spirit recurs in these four dances under the metaphors of the elements, wind and fire and earth and water. What we have here, I dare say, is a "phenomenology of spirit," Hegel's term, though far removed from Hegel's conceptual style. What we have instead in the four dances are conceptual metaphors of the spirit.

Recursion, Noam Chomsky and his colleagues have argued, "is the most important element of linguistic grammar, the only element that is entirely absent from all animal communication systems."[32] Let us consider spirit then, the inscape and the recursive element in my four dances, and let us see if spirit in the dances takes us beyond Hegel's conception of spirit as "pure self-identity within otherness."

My Dance of the Winds,

O guiding eye,
O guarding storm,
how can we know
the spirit from the wind?

echoes the words of Yeats about the dancer and the dance, but
also the words of Jesus to Nicodemus, "The wind blows where
it wills, and you hear the sound of it, but you do not know
whence it comes or whither it goes; so it is with every one
who is born of the Spirit" (John 3:8). The spirit, like the wind,
comes from the unknown and goes into the unknown, and so
does one "who is born of the Spirit," and so also in the Gospel
of John does Jesus who comes from God and goes to God.
There is a great circle here, coming from God the unknown
and going to God the unknown, "and you hear the sound of
it," and so it can be perceived and experienced.

There is an unknowing also in my Fire Dance,

O lonely wish,
impassioned hope,
how can we know
the spirit from the flame?

where I am echoing the words of Yeats and also the words de-
scribing the Pentecost, "a rushing mighty wind" and "cloven
tongues as of fire" and everyone "filled with the Holy Spirit"
and speaking "with other tongues as the Spirit gave them ut-
terance" (Acts 2:2–4). Jacques Derrida in his essay *Of Spirit*
is uneasy with the imagery of fire in Heidegger's thinking,
uneasy because of the Holocaust.[33] If we are thinking rather
of Pentecost and the kindling of the heart, we are thinking
like Tolkien of a call to "rekindle hearts in a world that grows
chill."[34]

In my Earth Dance,

O mystery that shows
and then withdraws,
how can we know
the spirit from the dance?

I am close to the original by Yeats, only instead of "the dancer" I have "the spirit." So the spirit is the dancer. What is more, I have the mystery showing and then withdrawing, the rhythm of the spirit's dance. Earth itself is not a metaphor of the spirit but the metaphor is rather the dance. I have taken this idea of showing and withdrawing from Heidegger, who says "That which shows itself and at the same time withdraws is the essential trait of what we call the mystery."[35] Spirit then is the mystery that shows itself and at the same time withdraws.

So in my River Dance,

O Spring of water
welling up into eternal life,
how can we know
the spirit from the thirst?

I pass from the mystery showing itself and withdrawing to the longing of the heart that is tantalized by the showing and withdrawing, and here I am echoing the words of Jesus to the woman at the well (John 4:14) and to those believing in him (John 7:35) about a spring of water within a person welling up into eternal life. Does the water of eternal life quench the thirst, or does the thirst itself, the transcendence of longing, become a spring of water welling up into eternal life?

Recursion is characteristic of spirit, according to Hegel, for spirit "returns to itself because it is pure self-identity within otherness."[36] So it makes sense from his point of view to say the thirst itself becomes a spring of water welling up into eternal life. But Hegel is turning away from transcendence to immanence and finding the whole reality of spirit in its return to itself. If we turn instead from immanence to transcendence, the longing is indeed a spring of water welling up into eternal life, but pointing beyond itself to the transcendent God. Thus "the soul is capable of God," *anima est capax Dei*, as Saint Thomas and Saint Augustine say,[37] but the soul is not God and is restless until it finds repose in God.

Spirit "returns to itself" also in our metaphors of spirit, wind and fire and earth and water. Consider the cycle of fire in Heraclitus, water and earth and fire and air, the reverse of my sequence of dances. We can interpret the cycle of fire, I have found, with the principle, "we can know more than we can tell," going from knowing to telling to unknowing to silence.[38] We can pass from immanence to transcendence, however, especially with the metaphor of the wind which "blows where it wills, and you hear the sound of it, but you do not know whence it comes or whither it goes" (John 3:8), for there the circle is from the unknown to the unknown, as in the words of the old Bedouin to Lawrence of Arabia, "The love is from God and of God and towards God."

Immanence, the indwelling presence of God in the world, if it is separated from transcendence, God being above and beyond the world, can mean "God dwells in you as you" as in Hinduism, or it can mean God coming to be in the world, as Hegel thought, or as was expressed most eloquently by Rilke in his *Letters to a Young Poet*, or more briefly in his *Stories of God*, as "He will be." All the same, Rilke also says in the same story "He *was*—at some time once *was*."[39] Immanence in Kant's philosophy means "within the realm of experience" and transcendence means "beyond the realm of experience." If we allow for *an experience of transcendence*, however, namely the transcendence of longing, how our heart's longing always goes beyond every finite object, how our heart is restless until it rests in God, we come to a transcendence that is not canceled out by immanence.

"Soul is capable of God" (*anima est capax Dei*), therefore, and the transcendence of longing points to the transcendence of God. This inner transcendence seems to be the inscape of the human being that becomes the inscape of words and music. It is "the mystery of music," as Steven Mithen calls it, speaking of the evolution of music and language, "a mystery explained but not diminished," as he says in conclusion.[40] He means the mystery of the origin of music and language, but I think the mystery is the transcendence of longing that finds expression in words and music. It is the restlessness of the heart's desire, ever seeking a repose that can only be found in God, a repose "which shows itself and at the same time withdraws," the dancing movement of dialectical thinking.

Dialectical thinking, like that of Hegel, as I understand it, contrasts especially with behavioral thinking. Instead of being shaped by our circumstances, as in behavioral thinking, we shape ourselves by *construing* our circumstances. Words and music then reflect our construing of our circumstances. The restless movement of heart's desire comes to rest in this construing, a "repose in light," as Joseph Joubert calls it in his *Notebooks*. "Wisdom is repose in light," he says, "for repose in light can be—tends to be—peace through light." Maurice Blanchot comments, "light that appeases and that gives peace, but repose in light is also repose—deprivation of all external help and impetus—so that nothing comes to disturb, or to pacify, the pure movement of light."[41]

Repose in light then becomes a kind of *rest in restlessness*,[42] I think, repose in the dancing movement of dialectical thinking, repose in the wind, the flame, the dance, the thirst of the spirit. It is like the poise of a whirling gyroscope. When I accept the restlessness of my heart, I come to rest in my restlessness. If we describe the restlessness of desire as a kind of perpetual motion, going from one image to another, what we have is something like *The Temptation of Saint Anthony* as described by Flaubert, memories and imaginings and visions, ending at last with Saint Anthony seeing the face of Christ in the rising sun.[43]

Rest in restlessness, if we think of it as repose in the wind, the flame, the dance, the thirst of the spirit, is repose in the dynamism of the heart's desire. I think of the words Max Gorky found in Tolstoy's diary, "God is my desire." When Gorky asked Tolstoy what he meant by that, Tolstoy said "I must have wanted to say 'God is my desire to know Him' . . . No, not that," and then he laughed and took the diary back from Gorky.[44] What comes to mind for me is Saint Augustine's prayer in his *Soliloquies*, "May I know me! May I know thee!" That is an expresssion of the heart's desire, to know me, to know thee. So to repose in heart's desire is to live in an *I and thou* with God.

An *I and thou* with God is the inside of the words in the Psalms, it seems, and of the words in the *Confessions* of Saint Augustine echoing the Psalms, and of the words set to music in Stravinsky's *Symphony of Psalms*. Thus too the defintion of song Saint Thomas gives is in his preface to the Psalms, "Song is the leap of mind in the eternal breaking out into sound." The eternal thus is the eternal *thou* in relation to the human *I*. Martin Buber in his essay *I and Thou* sees only the divine *thou* as the eternal in the relationship. Kierkegaard, on the other hand, speaking of "an eternal consciousness" in us, seems to imply an eternal *I and thou,* as if to say the human inscape is eternal in relation with the eternal *thou* of God.

Is it? Yes, if we conceive the human being as *an incarnate spirit,* if I say with Kierkegaard that by relating to myself and willing to be myself I am grounded transparently in God. For it is the transparent grounding in God, if anything, that makes the human spirit eternal. Hopkins, thinking of Duns Scotus and his teaching on haecceity or inscape, says of Duns Scotus's Oxford,

> these walls are what
> He haunted who of all men most sways my spirits to peace;
> Of realty the rarest-veined unraveller."[45]

The teaching on haecceity or thisness or inscape "most sways my spirits to peace," he is saying, for it implies an eternal consciousness, for "If there were no eternal consciousness in a man . . . what then would life be but despair?"

Inscape in us "sways my spirits to peace" if I think of inscape as an inner landscape opening onto the infinite. Spirit in my four dances seems to open onto the infinite,

O guiding eye,   O mystery that shows
O guarding storm,   and then withdraws,

O lonely wish,   O spring of water
impassioned hope,   welling up into eternal life.

Even Wittgenstein seems to have a sense of this opening onto infinity, "Our life is endless in the way that our visual field is without limit."[46] In life, it seems, as in logic and mathematics there are "the paradoxes of the infinite."

It is the question "How can we know the dancer from the dance?" that embodies the paradox in life. My own formulations of the question suggest an answer,

how can we know   how can we know
the spirit from the wind?   the spirit from the dance?

how can we know   how can we know
the spirit from the flame?   the spirit from the thirst?

If we think of the wind, the flame, the dance, the thirst as conceptual metaphors of the spirit, then the spirit is the answer, and the life of the spirit, the life of hope and peace and friends and intelligence.

Thus our phenomenology of spirit, if we can call it that, does not end in "absolute knowledge" like Hegel's, a knowing of knowing, but instead in a knowing of unknowing. It ends in inscape, the inner landscape of the human being opening onto the infinite. It ends therefore in the expression of inscape in story and song.

Story and Song

My name and yours, and the true name of the sun, or a spring of
water, or an unborn child, all are syllables of the great word
that is very slowly spoken by the shining of the stars.
—Ursula LeGuin

"In the beginning is the song," Michel Serres says in his
Genesis, and he contrasts this with "In the beginning was
the Word,"[1] but I think the Word can be the Song, as J. R. R.
Tolkien and C. S. Lewis tell the story of creation.[2] What I have
been saying about *theme* as the verbal inside of music and *inscape* as the musical inside of words can be realized in "the
great word that is very slowly spoken by the shining of the
stars,"[3] or we could say in the great word that is being *sung* by
the shining of the stars.

There is a considerable contrast between the story of creation as it is told in the Book of Genesis and the story of evolution as it is told in our times, for instance by Steven Mithen in
The Singing Neanderthals. There is a connection between the
telling of the life story and the telling of the story of creation,
for instance Saint Augustine ending his own life story in his

Confessions with the story of creation in Genesis, and Geronimo beginning his life story with the Apache story of creation or of the light coming into the darkness. As I see it, the telling of the life story is the key to the telling of the larger story. "The present type of order in the world has arisen from an unimaginable past," A. N. Whitehead says, "and it will find its grave in an unimaginable future."[4] Although he says "unimaginable," he is imagining a birth and a death, as in a life story.

If we see creation as a relationship rather than as a process, as a relationship of all things to God, then creation and evolution are compatible, though there is considerable contrast between them in storytelling. "We can know more than we can tell" suggests the difference between knowing the relationship and telling the story. When it comes to telling the story, however, the life story, as it is told in our times, reflects the emergence of an individual, where in earlier times it might have reflected the emergence of a people. Thus the stories in the Book of Genesis reflect the emergence of a people whereas the stories in a biography or autobiography reflect the emergence of an individual. Along with emergence there is separation, of a people from other peoples, of an individual from other individuals, and the separation seems to call for a reunion.

Reunion is a return to the beginning. I think again of the words of the old Bedouin to Lawrence of Arabia, "The love is from God and of God and towards God." Life and light and love, the three metaphors from the Gospel of John, all exist in this great circle, and story and song express the great circle in whole or in part. Let us consider the great circle then in the life story and the larger story, and the two questions the angels are said to ask when your soul leaves your body, "Where do you come from?" and "Where are you going?"

"Where do you come from?"

These two questions, "Where do you come from?" and "Where are you going?," are the questions that are posed in the Gospel of John. We answer the one with "remembrance of things past" and the other by "dreaming on things to come."[5] Yet if we are not only shaped by our circumstances, as in behavioral thinking, but shape ourselves by *construing* our circumstances, as in dialectical thinking, then our story is not simply of things happening to us but rather of us choosing and construing our lives. Construing comes of understanding, choosing comes of discovering the way. To say "I come from God, and I go to God" is a construing of my life, but it comes of the insight, "The love is from God and of God and towards God." What is more, "remembrance of things past" makes the great circle of life and light and love pass through "the particulars of my life."[6]

Time and memory, apart from the great circle of life and light and love, can seem opaque to eternity, but viewed in the great circle can seem translucent, even transparent to eternity. When Shakespeare speaks of "remembrance of things past" in his sonnet, he speaks mainly of losses and sorrows. If we distinguish between the person who lives the life and the life lived, then we can associate time with the life and eternity with the person. Losses and sorrows go with time and well-being and joy with eternity, as in Henry Vaughan's lines,

> I saw Eternity the other night,
> Like a great ring of pure and endless light,
> All calm, as it was bright.[7]

I associate eternity with the person and the great circle of life and light and love with eternity.

There is a "tension of essences" here, as in all storytelling, a tension between loss and sorrow on the one hand and well-being and joy on the other, a tension between time and eternity. "Tension of essences," Albert Lord says, is close to "free association."[8] It is this tension that allows the story to come out in different ways, happy-ending and sad-ending, and enables "the singer of tales," as Lord says, to tell the story in different ways. And we who are in the story don't know how it will come out, as Tolkien says, "You may know or guess what kind of a tale it is, happy-ending or sad-ending, but the people in it don't know. And you don't want them to."[9] What we can know, being in the story, is the tension of essences.

What I said before is "we can know more than we can tell." We can tell the story, but we can know the relationship, the *I and it* and the *I and thou* and the *I in them and thou in me.* To know the relationship is to know the tension of essences. In those questions "Where do you come from?" and "Where are you going?" the tension of essences is a tension of meanings, as in the words "The wind blows where it wills, and you hear the sound of it, but cannot tell where it comes from and where it goes: so is everyone who is born of the Spirit" (John 3:8).

Et in Arcadia ego, "And I was in Arcadia," the motto of Goethe's *Italian Journey,* a tomb inscription, often depicted in classical painting, has a similar tension of meanings. Goethe apparently meant that his Italian journey was for him a journey into Arcadia. I used the saying as the epigraph of a chapter, "An Italian Journey," in my memoir *A Journey with God in Time.*[10] It answers the question "Where are you coming from in your Italian journey?" Goethe was shaking off a romantic for a classical vision. I was simply learning from my encounter with ancient Rome, with Renaissance Rome, and with modern Rome. If "we can know more than we can tell," it is, as Polanyi says, by dwelling in the particulars of what we know, and that indwelling in particulars, I have come to think, is the method of the Renaissance, "the method of Leonardo da Vinci," as Paul Valery calls it, the method of *ostinato rigore.*[11] What then of the great circle of life and light and love, how does it pass through the particulars, through "the particulars of my life"?

To go from a romantic to a classical vision, as Goethe did, was to go from loss and sorrow, as in his *Sorrows of Young Werther,* to well-being and joy, as in the words Martin Buber quotes from Goethe as the epigraph of *I and Thou,* "So waiting, I have won from you the end: God's presence in each element."[12] There is a hint there of how the great circle of life and light and love passes through the particulars of a life, "God's presence in each element" and also "I have won from you." To go from loss and sorrow to well-being and joy, as we have been saying, is to go from time to eternity. For Buber it is to go from *I and it* to *I and thou* ("I have won from you"); for Goethe it is to come into God's presence in nature ("in each element"); for me it is to come to realize "We all have within us a center of stillness surrounded by silence."

If we say with Plato time is "a changing image of eternity," then time is a changing image of *I and thou*, as in Buber's thinking, a changing image of God's presence in nature, as in Goethe's thinking, the path, I would say, taken by the quiet eye of the moving storm of time. Goethe's method, as in his autobiography *Poetry and Truth in My Life,* is to turn the truth of life into poetry; Leonardo's is to turn the truth of life into art; Saint Augustine's is to turn the truth of life into prayer. If we think, though, of the human body in relation to the body of the world in Leonardo, and of the human soul in relation to the soul of the world in Goethe, and of the body in relation to the soul in Augustine, we find a convergence. "Where do you come from?" and "Where are you going?" both point to the transcendental home. "Time can become constitutive only when connection with the transcendental home has been lost."[13]

"Once upon a time," as stories begin, can still be said if time is constitutive, but it becomes more literal, as things do when time becomes opaque to eternity. The symbolic life seems to be characteristic of *homo sapiens,* and its impairment in a matter-of-fact mentality seems to be a regression. Storytelling takes its origin in imagination, as Padraic Colum says in his essay on storytelling, quoting George Bernard Shaw, "Imagination is the beginning of creation: you imagine what you desire, you will what you imagine, and finally you create what you will."[14] Observe, though, that desire is the actual beginning, "you imagine what you desire."

What is the desire that gives rise to storytelling? "Within our whole universe the story only has authority to answer that cry of heart of its characters," Isak Dinesen says, "that one cry of heart of each of them: *Who am I?*"[15] That cry of heart gives rise to our two questions, "Where do you come from?" and "Where are you going?" That cry of heart is an expression of what I call *the heart's desire.* The answer to the cry of heart is the life story but also the larger story in which the life story is set. It is what Robert Jay Lifton calls "the symbolic integration of a life."[16] Thus if I see my own life as a journey with God in time, I am seeing it also in the larger story of "God with us" (Matthew 1:23). Thus who I am is linked with who God is for me, as in Saint Augustine's prayer "May I know me! May I know thee!" This would hold true even for someone to whom "God is dead."

It is true, someone to whom "God is dead" will not be able to pray "May I know me! May I know thee!" I think again of a friend who had not been able to pray for years, and then was able to pray again after I gave him to read *Stories of God* by Rilke. I am supposing this helped by getting him out of a matter-of-fact mentality and into the symbolic life that underlies the symbolic integration of a life in a life story and a larger story that encompasses the life story. A storyless life is perhaps what Thoreau had in mind when he spoke in *Walden* of people living lives of "quiet desperation."[17]

There is an answer to "quiet desperation" in that motto *Et in Arcadia ego,* "And I was in Arcadia." And I was in Italy six years studying, and I was learning to love with all my mind, reading and coming to peace of mind, coming to a peaceful vision of everyone and everything coming from God and returning to God. It was an intellectual Arcadia. "There were traces of him everywhere," Rilke says in *Stories of God.* "In all the pictures I found bits of his smile, the bells were still alive with his voice, and on the statues I recognized the imprint of his hands."[18] The presence of God was there for me too, but especially in the peaceful vision of the great circle of life and light and love.

A peaceful vision—it is like "the simplicity of vision" that Pierre Hadot ascribes to Plotinus—the One, the emanation of all from the One, and the return of all to the One.[19] Thus it is like a classical vision, as is Goethe's. Yet it is also a vision of the great circle described in the Gospel of John, a circle that can be found also in the parables of Jesus, such as the Parable of the Prodigal Son, who goes out from the Father and then comes back to the Father. "Now that I can see it all as from a lonely hilltop, I know it was the story of a mighty vision given to a man too weak to use it," Black Elk says of his life. "But if the vision was true and mighty, as I know, it is true and mighty yet," he says, "for such things are of the spirit, and it is in the darkness of their eyes that men get lost."[20]

Spirit is relatedness, as I understand it, and the life of the spirit is a life of hope and peace and friends and intelligence. A life of faith, I am thinking, is a life of spirit, "seeing light with your heart when all your eyes see is darkness." A vision of the great circle of life and light and love is "seeing light with your heart," and "when all your eyes see is darkness" is "the darkness of their eyes" in which "men get lost." The light and the darkness are both part of the total vision, as Black Elk saw his people walking two roads, a red one, "the road of good," and a black, "a fearful road, a road of troubles and war."[21] So too the great circle of life and light and love in the Gospel of John belongs to the light shining in the darkness, "and the darkness comprehended it not" (John 1:5), or in another translation, "and the darkness has not overshadowed it."[22]

How are we to conceive the darkness or the relation of the light and the darkness? Are they two roads, as in Black Elk's vision, the red road and the black road, "the road of good" and "a fearful road, a road of troubles and war"? And is there a choice to be made between them, as in Deuteronomy, "I have set before you life and death, blessing and cursing: therefore choose life that both thou and thy seed may live" (Deuteronomy 30:19)? I suppose this is the point of Kierkegaard's *Either/Or.* To choose life would be to choose life and light and love, to choose to live in the great circle of life and light and love.

There is a far point on the great circle, nevertheless, where "Even love must pass through loneliness," as Wendell Berry says,[23] where even light must pass through darkness, we could say too, where even life must pass through death. "Men perish," Alcmaeon, an early Greek philosopher, said, "because they cannot join the beginning to the end."[24] We get lost in loneliness and darkness and death from being unable to join the beginning to the end. The answer then is to find the beginning, "Where do you come from?" and to join that to the end, "Where are you going?" In the vision of the great circle of life and light and love thus "In my beginning is my end," as T.S. Eliot says, and "In my end is my beginning."[25] What is the beginning, therefore, and what is the end?

In the Word is the beginning and the end, we could say, echoing the opening words of the Gospel of John, "In the beginning was the Word," and the closing words of *The Death of Virgil* by Hermann Broch, "it was the word beyond speech."[26] To say the beginning and the end is in the Word is to place the life story within a larger encompassing story. Does thinking back, *andenken* as Heidegger calls it, carry us back to a beginning in the Word? "Thinking is thanking" can take us back far enough to say with Dag Hammarskjöld "For all that has been—Thanks!" And if our thinking is indeed thanking, if it is prayer, that is, it can take us all the way back to the Word in the beginning.

What then is the relation of the life story to the larger story of beginning and ending in the Word? I suppose simply "Thanks!" and "Yes!," as in Dag Hammarskjöld's *Markings,* "For all that has been—Thanks! To all that shall be—Yes!," for by that "Thanks!" and "Yes!" I enter into the great circle of life and light and love. "Thinking is thanking" can carry me along the lines of the great circle without assuming too much about my personal destiny. I enter into the relationship of Jesus with God, making his God my God, making his Father my Father, without thereby assuming with Meister Eckhart that whatever is said of him can be said also of me.

This is what I call *participation*, using a term from Saint Thomas Aquinas that goes all the way back to Plato (*methexis*).[27] If I participate in the relationship of Jesus with his God and Father, I enter into a personal relationship with the Absolute. All the same, I cannot say, as he does "I came forth from the Father, and am come into the world: again, I leave the world, and go to the Father" (John 16:28). Instead, I have my own origin and end in time. Still, I participate in his coming from God and his going to God, having a personal relationship with the Absolute. I think of the title scene of Tolstoy's *War and Peace*, where Prince Andre, lying on his back, experiences peace in the midst of war, looking up into the sky from the battlefield of Austerlitz.[28] Thus too "We all have within us a center of stillness surrounded by silence," as Dag Hammarskjöld says, and so I too can experience eternity in the midst of time.

If time and eternity are dimensions of life, time the horizontal dimension associated with the life from birth to death, eternity the vertical dimension associated with the person living the life, then I have an origin and end in time and also an origin and end in eternity. So I can say "I come from God, and I go to God," speaking of my origin and end in eternity, but it can also be said "Dust thou art, and unto dust shalt thou return" (Genesis 3:19), speaking of my origin and end in time.

Time is "a changing image of eternity," as Plato says, and that seems to reveal the connection between my origin and end in time and my origin and end in eternity. Paul Griffiths in his *Concise History of Western Music* (2006) describes each stage of music history in terms of time, "Time whole, Time measured 1100–1400, Time sensed 1400–1630, Time known 1690–1770, Time embraced 1770–1815, Time escaping 1815–1907, Time tangled 1908–1975, and Time lost 1975–."[29] Time for him is the key to the story of music, as for Heidegger it is the key to the story of philosophy. If we describe music too as "a changing image of eternity," we are ready for an insight into image that will answer our question "Where are you going?"

Of ancient music such as plainsong Griffiths says "Time is whole" and "It is not going anywhere. It is there."[30] I think of Wittgenstein saying "If by eternity is understood not endless temporal duration but timelessness, then he lives eternally who lives in the present."[31] To speak of "time whole" is like speaking of "timelessness." It comes down to *living in the present.* If we speak instead of *living in the presence,* then indeed time is whole but it is going somewhere, going from the past into the future. I think for instance of the concluding sentence of the Gospel of Matthew, "I am with you always, even unto the end of the world." What is expressed there is an abiding presence, but it is going somewhere, "even unto the end of the world." I see plainsong this way, as expressing a living in the presence rather than simply a living in the present.

When we go from living in the presence to living in time, then time is no longer *transparent* to eternity but at most *translucent,* sometimes even *opaque* to eternity. That is how time appears in the history of Western music, as Griffiths tells the story. If we set the story in the larger story of the human race, starting with the emergence and separation of peoples, and going on from there to the emergence and separation of the individual, the story of Western music reflects especially this last, the emergence and separation of the individual, the individual composer, the individual performer, even the individual listener. This emergence and separation, however, points on toward a reunion, a reunion of the individual with humanity, even a reunion of humanity with God, and that reunion would be the future of music. So plainsong is the past but something like plainsong may also be the future.

I think of the mystic road of love, "the road of the union of love with God" (*el camino de la union del amor con Dios*) that Saint John of the Cross describes in *The Dark Night of the Soul.*[32] Maybe we have to go through a dark night in which "God is dead" to reach "the union of love with God." Hegel took that sentence "God is dead" from a Good Friday hymn and gave it new significance to describe the "infinite grief" and the "absolute suffering" of the "Golgotha of absolute spirit."[33] It sounds a bit overly dramatic, but it does seem to describe a real experience of the present time that we seem to be going through ("Godless Europe"). If we can read the experience more with Saint John of the Cross than with Hegel, we can find some hope in it of going through what Saint John calls *una noche dichosa,* "a happy night" or perhaps "a fortunate night," in that it is leading us on "the road of the union of love with God."

If we see the emergence and separation we have undergone, first of peoples and then of individuals, as leading onto a road of union or reunion, we are envisioning a great circle in time of life and light and love. The circle is there in the life story and also in the larger story, "A way a lone a last a loved a long the riverrun."[34] Just as we say "living in the presence" rather than simply "living in the present," though, so also we can say of the circle that it is "from God and of God and toward God."

If the road into the future in the life story and the larger story is "the road of the union of love with God," then as Shakespeare says in his sonnet,

> Not mine own fears, nor the prophetic soul
> Of the wide world, dreaming on things to come,
> Can yet the lease of my true love control,
> Suppos'd as forfeit to a confin'd doom.[35]

Not my own apprehensions nor the sad wisdom of the world at large can envisage an end to my love, supposedly limited by my mortality, he is saying. And that would be even truer of "the union of love with God." To speak of the great circle of life and light and love and of "the road of the union of love with God" is to speak of eternal life, and yet there are "mine own fears" and "the prophetic soul of the wide world."

"If the doors of perception were cleansed," William Blake says, "everything would appear as it is, infinite."[36] This is what I mean when I say the inscape, the inner landscape of the human being, opens onto infinity. Duns Scotus speaks of the "thisness" (*haecceitas*) of the human being and of the infinity of God, and this seems to be the connexion, the inner landscape of the human being opening onto the infinity of God. Eternal life then is not something inhuman, something foreign to a human being. "If the doors of perception were cleansed," we would perceive not only the horizontal dimension of life, going from birth to death, but also the vertical dimension, pointing into infinity, like Prince Andre lying on the battlefield in *War and Peace*, looking up into the sky.

"How was it I did not see that lofty sky before?" he says. "And how happy I am to have found it at last. Yes! All is vanity, all is a cheat, except that infinite sky. There is nothing, nothing but that. But even that is not, there is nothing but peace and stillness. And thank God! . . ."[37] When the doors of perception are cleansed, we come to something like this, a perception of the vertical dimension of life opening onto infinity. At first it is literally a vertical dimension, looking up into the sky, but then it becomes a metaphor of peace in the midst of war, "there is nothing but peace and stillness." It is the inner peace and stillness of "we all have within us a center of stillness surrounded by silence." It is the eternal in us, passing through time.

Living in the horizontal dimension means living toward death; living in the vertical dimension means living toward life. I think again of that passage in Deuteronomy, "I have set before you life and death, blessing and cursing: therefore choose life that both thou and thy seed may live" (Deuteronomy 30:19). It is true, we live in both dimensions, toward death and toward life. To go from "being toward death," as Heidegger calls it, to "freedom toward death," however, I think we must learn to live toward life, toward eternal life. I realize if you accept death then you become free, but how do you come to accept death if you have not discovered the eternal in us?

There are two ways of passing through time, according to Jung, one is to walk through upright, the other is to be dragged through. Walking through upright, I take it, involves being conscious of the vertical dimension passing through the horizontal, thus the image of walking through vertical or upright. Being dragged through involves being conscious only of the horizontal dimension, thus the image of being dragged through horizontal. "Everything which belongs to an individual's life shall enter into it," Jung says, defining what he means by "individuation."[38] For him then walking through upright is conscious and willing individuation, being dragged through is unconscious individuation. I would add that for everything that belongs to my life to enter into it consciously, I have to be conscious of the eternal in us.

There is a goal, according to Jung, toward which you are being dragged or walking upright, and the goal is wholeness. I think of the great commandment, to love "with all your heart, and with all your soul, and with all your might" (Deuteronomy 6:4), and the phrase that is added in the Gospels, "with all your mind" (Matthew 22:37, Mark 12:30, Luke 10:27). It is a formula of wholeness, and it seems to imply that life is about learning to love. "Love? What is love?" Prince Andre thinks on his deathbed in *War and Peace*. "Love hinders death. Love is life. All, all that I understand, I understand only because I love. All is, all exists only because I love. All is bound up in love alone. Love is God, and dying means for me a particle of love, to go back to the universal and eternal source of love."[39] Here again we have the great circle of life and light and love.

What does it mean "to go back to the universal and eternal source of love"? Asking that question, "A man would know the end he goes to, but he cannot know it if he does not turn, and return to his beginning, and hold that beginning in his being."[40] I suppose you do this by thinking back to the beginning, where "thinking is thanking." I think of Virgil on his deathbed, thinking back to the Word in the beginning, "it was the word beyond speech," or Don Quixote on his deathbed, thinking back to his true identity, "I was mad but now I am sane," or Prince Andre on his deathbed, thinking back to "the universal and eternal source of love."

These instances, it is true, are all fictional, but they describe the common experience of facing death and seeing one's life pass before one in review. "Thanks!" and "Yes!" like that of Dag Hammarskjöld at the turning point of his life seems appropriate also for facing death. "If the doors of perception were cleansed everything would appear as it is, infinite," even life itself in the face of death. I think of a friend in his last days, dying of cancer, saying you have a choice between resentment and thanksgiving, and himself making the choice for thanksgiving, as in "For all that has been—Thanks!" Even on the deathbed, we could say, "thinking is thanking."

Is eternal life all retrospect then, or is it something more, a vision of God? Eternal longing is longing of mind and heart and soul. I imagine the vision of God as corresponding to the longing, a peace of mind, a peace of heart, a peace of soul, and so essentially an inward peace. It would be something we already have within ourselves in that "we all have within us a center of stillness surrounded by silence." The idea of eternal life in the Gospel of John seems to be something that begins already in this life on earth, and that would correspond to our center of stillness. What is specifically Christian about it would be the relationship with God, "my Father and your Father, my God and your God," that constitutes the peace.

"It is for those who come here to fill the void with what they find in their center of stillness," Dag Hammarskjöld says at the end of his brochure for the Meditation Room at the UN, having begun by saying "We all have within us a center of stillness surrounded by silence." The center of stillness seems to be something universal and common to all human beings. "What they find in their center of stillness," on the other hand, seems to be something more specific to each person and to each spiritual tradition. The relationship with God that Jesus speaks of to Mary Magdalen in the Gospel of John, "my Father and your Father, my God and your God," describes what followers of Christ can find in their center of stillness.

Passing over to other religions and coming back with new insight to my roots in Christianity, I find the idea of eternal life a common one in the higher religions. What is special to

Christianity is the personal relation with the Absolute, the intimacy of Jesus with the God he calls Abba. If I enter into that intimacy, as I am invited to do in Christianity, I find myself in a personal relationship with God. "You can have a personal relationship with the Absolute," as a Vietnamese friend of mine told me who had converted to Catholicism from Buddhism. "You can be a friend of God, even a lover of God." Eternal life then, from this point of view, is a "union of love with God," and the way to eternal life is "the road of the union of love with God" that Saint John of the Cross describes, passing through the trial of faith he calls "the dark night of the soul."

There is a trial of faith both in the life story and in the larger story. I think again of Saint Thérèse of Lisieux. There is a chapter called "The Trial of Faith (1896–1897)" in her *Story of a Soul* where she says the darkness seems to say to her "You are dreaming about the light, about a fatherland embalmed in the sweetest perfumes; you are dreaming about the eternal possession of the Creator of all these marvels; you believe that one day you will walk out of this fog which surrounds you! Advance, advance; rejoice in death which will give you not what you hope for but a night still more profound, the night of nothingness."[41] I think again of that saying "Faith is seeing light with your heart when all your eyes see is darkness." Her eyes are seeing darkness here, but her heart is seeing light.

"Laughing lions must come," Nietzsche says, seeing that same darkness.[42] You are not laughing, though, when you see light with your heart, but you are facing death and darkness with hope. The saying of Heraclitus, "If one does not hope, one will not find the unhoped-for, since there is no trail leading to it and no path,"[43] leaves us with the thought of "the unhoped-for," which could be, as in Saint Thérèse's trial of faith, "not what you hope for but a night still more profound, the night of nothingness." To see light with your heart, nevertheless, is to see light rather than darkness. It is like the light shining in the darkness in the prologue of John. Each translation of that verse is significant here, "And the light shines in the darkness, and the darkness did not comprehend it (KJ), did not overcome it (RSV), did not overshadow it" (Peter Levi).

What is this darkness that does not comprehend the light, that does not overcome the light, that does not overshadow the light? Apparently it is the darkness of unbelief. On the other hand, the light is like physical light traveling through the darkness of space, unseen except when it encounters and illumines an object. Seeing light with your heart, therefore, when all your eyes see is darkness is faith, a willingness to die and yet a hope to live, a willingness to walk alone and yet and hope to walk unalone. "The dark night of the soul" thus is not the darkness of unbelief but the darkness of the trial of faith, the darkness of unknowing, "the cloud of unknowing in the which a soul is oned with God." It is like the unseen light traveling through the darkness of outer space, unseen until it encounters and illumines an object.

Illumining the mind and kindling the heart, that is what the light does, shining in the darkness. It is shining in the darkness of unbelief, as in the prayer "Lord, I believe; help thou mine unbelief" (Mark 9:24). If I pray this prayer, I am inviting the light into the darkness of my life. Consider the darkness: anguish and abandonment and despair (as Sartre describes them in his essay *Existentialism Is a Humanism*).[44] If I invite the light into the darkness of my life, I am inviting the light of faith, of willingness and hope, into the darkness of anguish and abandonment and despair. I am indeed seeing light with my heart when all my eyes see is the darkness of my life. "Lord, I believe," embracing willingness and hope, while praying "help thou mine unbelief."

Our two questions "Where do you come from?" and "Where are you going?" are answered by the great circle of life and light and love, "The love is from God and of God and towards God." The circle goes through a far point, though, where love passes through loneliness, and light passes through darkness, and life passes through death, and at that far point it can seem in the trial of faith that "God is dead." That seems to be where we are now in the larger story, "dark times" as Hannah Arendt says in her *Men in Dark Times*.[45] Our "blessed assurance" of faith, nevertheless, is that the darkness does not comprehend, does not overcome, does not overshadow the light.

Eternal Consciousness

If there were no eternal consciousness in a man . . . what then
would life be but despair?
—Kierkegaard

Eternal consciousness is an answer to "quiet desperation," as in Thoreau's saying, "The mass of men lead lives of quiet desperation."[1] And I suppose this is what Kierkegaard meant saying "If there were no eternal consciousness in a man . . . what then would life be but despair?"[2] Kierkegaard says it in *Fear and Trembling,* writing about faith, but he spells it out in *Sickness unto Death,* writing about the opposite of faith, namely despair. If we think of faith, as we have been doing, as a combination of willingness and hope, then the opposite of faith is unwillingness and despair. Willingness here is willingness to die, and hope is hope to live. Again, willingness is willingness to walk alone and hope is hope to walk unalone. So what is eternal consciousness?

It is, I take it, consciousness of the eternal in us. If time is "a changing image of eternity," as Plato says, the changing image of the human being is like *The Voyage of Life,* four paintings by

Thomas Cole, showing childhood, youth, adulthood, and age.[3] The eternal in us is the person going through these phases. It is the vertical dimension of the life, as in the title scene of *War and Peace* where Prince Andre lay on the battlefield looking up into the peaceful sky, perceiving peace in the midst of war. If the horizontal dimension is time and the vertical dimension is eternity, then eternal consciousness is awareness of the vertical dimension. What is more, the vertical dimension carries through the horizontal, as the person walks through life upright instead of being dragged through in "quiet desperation." Willingness and hope, accordingly, is willingness to walk through upright with hope in the face of death and darkness.

"If I must die someday, what can I do to fulfill my desire to live?" That is how I originally formulated the problem of death in my first book, *The City of the Gods*. I found that each human society had its own characteristic solution of the problem of death, such as doing memorable deeds or running the gamut of experience or simply becoming free to live and to love by accepting death. The true answer to death, I came to believe, was in "the words of eternal life" (John 6:68). This led on to a realization that eternal life begins already in this life on earth, and so the question is not so much a life after death as a deeper life now, a life of the spirit that can endure death and survive it. Thus the "eternal consciousness" of this book.

Originally I was going to call this book *A Tension of Essences*, as Albert Lord calls the tension in a story that allows it to come out to a happy or a sad ending.[4] After writing the first chapter on "We can know more than we can tell" in telling the story, and coming to the second, "Is matter a dimension?," I saw again the role of death in the story, "If there were no eternal consciousness in a man," as Kierkegaard says, "what then would life be but despair?" I saw that it is eternal consciousness in us that gives rise to a tension of essences in storytelling.

A tension of essences is the sort of thing Dickens formulates in the opening sentence of *A Tale of Two Cities*, "It was the best of times, it was the worst of times. . . ."[5] The basic tension is between time and eternity, between the horizontal dimension of time and the vertical dimension of eternity, as in the title scene of *War and Peace* where Prince Andre, lying on the battlefield, looks up into the infinite peaceful sky and perceives peace in the midst of war. It is a tension that appears both in the life story, as in the *Confessions* of Saint Augustine, and in the larger story, as in his *City of God*. When it comes to the question Tolkien poses, "I wonder what sort of a tale we've fallen into?" the answer seems to be that we know the tension of essences but not the outcome, happy or sad. "I wonder," he has Frodo say to Sam, "but I don't know. And that's the way of a real tale. Take any one you're fond of. You may know or guess what kind of a tale it is, happy-ending or sad-ending, but the people in it don't know. And you don't want them to."[6]

What then of Polanyi's principle, "We can know more than we can tell"? If the tension of essences in the story is essentially a tension between time and eternity, "We can know more than we can tell" means we can tell the story but we can know our relationship with time and eternity. There is *the moment*, as Kierkegaard describes it, a timeless point in our inner subjectivity when we freely enact our relationship with eternity. And there is a secular version of the same thing in Heidegger's thinking when you freely enact your relationship with time, going from "being toward death" to an impassioned "freedom toward death," like my student who told me "I've found it! I've found it!" and when I asked what he had found told me "You accept death, and then you're free!"

If we see time as "a changing image of eternity," then our relationship with time is also a relationship with eternity. Willingness and hope, the combination that is faith, is a willingness to die and yet a hope to live. The hope and the life are pervasive, "Where there is life there is hope" and vice-versa where there is hope there is life, just as the passing of things and the death is pervasive. Eternal life is "more than we can tell" in telling the life story, and also in telling the larger story. Yet "We can know" insofar as we can know the relationship with God, as in "I know whom I have believed" (2 Timothy 1:12).

There is knowing and unknowing. On the one hand, "I know whom I have believed," and on the other there is "The cloud of unknowing in the which a soul is oned with God." The knowing is of the relationship with God, the *I and thou* with God. The unknowing is of *I* and of *thou*, "May I know me! May I know thee!" There is mystery, therefore, and the mystery "shows itself and at the same time withdraws,"[7] shows in knowing and withdraws in unknowing. Here again we come upon "a tension of essences." The tension in "I know whom I have believed" is between "I know" and "I have believed." There is the willingness and the hope in the believing, and there is the knowing that comes of believing, as Saint Augustine says, "I desired to see with my understanding that which I believed."[8] By accepting the unknowing in believing I come to know, to understand, to see light with my heart when all my eyes see is darkness.

If spirit returns to itself, as Hegel says,[9] going from being before others to being before self to being before God, then the knowing and the unknowing is a returning. Matter situates spirit, I have been saying, arguing that matter is a dimension, that the brain situates the mind, that the body situates the soul. If spirit returns to itself in knowing and unknowing, it is matter that situates the return. A materialist point of view would equate the mind with the brain and would obscure the return. Spirit is relatedness, to others and to self and to God, and if we recognize relatedness, we have to let go of materialist reductions like Feuerbach's "Man is what he eats" (which sounds more witty in German, *Der Mensch ist, was er isst*).[10]

Returning to itself, the human spirit comes to recollection and to "emotion recollected in tranquillity," the origin of poetry according to Wordsworth. If the brain situates the mind, as I have been arguing, then the brain situates memory, as in the memory theatres or memory palaces of the Renaissance. In present-day biology of mind the human brain itself is the memory theatre or the memory palace, as in Eric Kandel's work described in his book *In Search of Memory*.[11] If we compare the present-day biology of mind with something like *The*

Memory Palace of Matteo Ricci described by Jonathan Spence,[12] the symbols in the Renaissance memory theatre or memory palace appear to be replaced by the facts in the present-day biology of mind. Situating the facts of memory and situating the symbols of memory, however, may prove to be one and the same thing.

There are facts about neurons and the storing of memory but the *content* of memory is on the order of "emotion recollected in tranquillity," the origin of poetry. "The secret of Truth is as follows," João Ubaldo Ribeiro says in the epigraph of his book *An Invincible Memory,* "there are no facts, there are only stories."[13] What he is talking about is the *content* of memory, but it remains true that "We can know more than we can tell," and so there is more than stories in our knowing. All the same, he does have a point, that the basic content of memory is symbolic, not facts but stories. "Insight into image," as my teacher Bernard Lonergan used to say, is the way to knowledge.[14] If the content of memory is symbolic, consisting of images, the content of knowing or understanding is something more. What is that something more? I would say *relationships.*

Matter situating spirit, the brain situating the mind, the body situating the soul, that too is relationship. If I say spirit is relatedness, I am saying it is not only relatedness of person to person, person to self, and person to God, but also relatedness to matter, to the brain, to the body. It is relatedness to the things of life entering and passing from the life. Hegel's definition of spirit, "pure self-identity within otherness,"[15] seems to refer primarily to the passage from relating to others to relating to self, and his dialectic is the process of coming to oneself. Thinking of the human being as an incarnate spirit, however, I would include all forms of relatedness. As E. M. Forster says in *Howard's End,* "Only connect!"[16]

Coming to oneself and coming to God, nevertheless, is the journey of the spirit in time, "May I know me! May I know thee!" As I understand it, the journey goes from being before others to being before oneself to being before God. The standpoint before others is like that of Newman in his *Apologia,* that before self is like that of Saint Augustine in his *Soliloquies,* and that before God is like that of Saint Augustine in his *Confessions.* Hegel's *Phenomenology of Spirit* records his own spiritual journey, his "voyage of discovery" as he calls it,[17] and he goes through these stages, but after the third stage he speaks of "absolute knowledge," and what he seems to understand by that is *a knowing of knowing* like Aristotle's notion of God, but it seems to amount really to the standpoint before self, "pure self-identity within otherness."

Although Newman in his *Apologia* speaks from the standpoint before others, it is clear that he lives not only in that standpoint but also in the standpoint before self and before God, as when he speaks of being "alone with the Alone" (*solus cum solo*).[18] It is when a person is living in the standpoint before others without any awareness of a more comprehensive standpoint before self and before God that there can be what Hegel describes as the dialectic of the masters and the slaves. If I am living in the hope of acceptance and the fear of rejection that arise in the standpoint before others, I am vulnerable in my hope and my fear to the kind of thing Otto Rank describes when he speaks of the confusion in modern relationships between human needs and spiritual needs, and says "It is just as unbearable to be God as it is to be an utter slave."[19]

Coming to myself means coming to "emotion recollected in tranquillity." It means being relieved of the burden of hope and fear when the hope and fear are "recollected in tranquillity" at the end of the day, when I am writing, for instance, in a diary. I come then to Saint Augustine's prayer in his *Soliloquies,* "May I know me! May I know thee!" I come to what Pierre Hadot calls "the inner citadel," speaking of Marcus Aurelius writing at the end of the day in his *Meditations,* even at the end of the day on the battlefield.[20] All the same, I do not think of this recollection as a knowing of knowing like Hegel but as a knowing of unknowing that can be expressed in a prayer to know myself and to know God. That is why the standpoint before self is not final but leads on to a standpoint before God.

If we can go from stories of God to prayer, we can come into a standpoint before God. But how? One way would be by "rethinking the ontological argument"[21] or one of the other classical arguments for the existence of God. But this would be to engage in a quest of certainty, and that I believe always leads to greater uncertainty and more intense doubt. Another way is to go on a quest of understanding, where insight consists of reasons of the heart becoming known to the mind. That is the way of faith, "seeing light with your heart when all your eyes see is darkness." It is "faith seeking understanding," then, which is what Saint Anselm had in mind when he first proposed the ontological argument.[22] And that quest of understanding allows us to go from stories of God to prayer.

Going from stories of God to prayer is what is happening in the Psalms where "song," as Saint Thomas Aquinas says, "is the leap of mind in the eternal breaking out into sound." You can hear that leap of mind (*exultatio mentis*) in the *Laudate* and the *Alleluia* of Stravinsky's *Symphony of Psalms*. Of the four memories that Yeats speaks of in *A Vision*, the memory of past lives, the memory of moments of exaltation, the memory of the events of one's present life, and the memory of ideas displayed by persons,[23] it is the memory of moments of exaltation that is above all "emotion recollected in tranquillity" and expressed in song defined in this way. I think of an inscription on a German opera house,

> Bach gave us God's word.
> Mozart gave us God's laughter.
> Beethoven gave us God's fire.
> God gave us music
> that we might pray without words.

There is prayer with words and prayer without words, as there is music with words and music without words. There is a musical inside of words, I believe, and a verbal inside of music, and so words and music are related, I think, as are the two hemispheres of the brain. If we think of the brain as situating the mind, we can think of the two hemispheres as situating words and music. Theme, the musical theme, Wagner's *Leitmotiv*, is the verbal inside of music, and inscape, as Hopkins names it, is the musical inside of words.

Musical themes, as Wagner conceived them, are "motifs of memory."[24] If we connect musical themes with the four memories that Yeats describes, we have the memory of moments of exaltation that is primary in song as "the leap of mind in the eternal breaking out into sound," but we also have the memory of the events of life, of past lives, and of ideas displayed by persons. If music can give expression to all four memories, then there is some kind of equivalence between music and language. It is true, music like poetry takes its origin in "emotion recollected in tranquillity." So the equivalence with language is essentially an equivalence of music and poetry. Thus the ancient word *musica* in Latin and *musike* in Greek signifies music and poetry. And so I want to speak of a unity of words and music that I call "the music of words."

Inscape, as the musical inside of words, is the inner landscape of words opening onto infinity. It is clear how that connects with the heart restless until it rests in God, but how does it connect with music? I suppose the music is in what Hopkins speaks of as the *once* and *oftening* and *over-and-overing* and *aftering* of inscape.[25] There are "the words of eternal life" (John 6:68), and out of these words come the concept of "the Word of life" (1 John 1:1), the Word in the beginning (John 1:1), and I would add, the Word in the end, thinking of the last words in *The Death of Virgil* by Hermann Broch, "it was the word beyond speech."[26] Inscape then is a general term but the primary inscape, I would say, is that of "the words of eternal life." This above all is an inner landscape opening onto infinity.

Telling the story then of a life, and telling the larger story encompassing the life story, "we can know more than we can tell" insofar as we can know this inner landscape opening onto infinity. One way of seeing this inner landscape and its opening onto infinity is to see our story as the story of God, our coming to be as God's coming to be in us. That is the way Hegel sees it in his *Phenomenology of Spirit,* and that is the way Rilke sees it in his *Letters to a Young Poet.* "Why do you not think of him as the coming one, immanent from all eternity," Rilke says to the young poet, "the future one, the final fruit of the tree whose leaves we are?"[27] This is a heterodox view if we think of God not being until he comes to be in us, but an orthodox view if we think of God being in eternity and coming to be in us in time.

Time and eternity, that is the relation we are considering here, speaking of our story and the story of God. If we say with Plato that time is "a changing image of eternity," then our story in time is a changing image of God. What is the story of God? As Rilke tells it in his *Stories of God,* it is the story of the past and the present and the future, as if to say,

> Once God was.
> Is God now?
> God will be![28]

This reflects the great circle of love that I have been speaking of, the circle coming from God and going to God, but passing through a far point where "Even love must pass through loneliness." As for the existence of God, as Kierkegaard says, "when I let the proof go, the existence is there."[29]

As I understand it, letting the proof go is letting go of a quest of certainty and going over to a quest of understanding. "Once God was" comes of a search for God in time and memory, "Is God now?" is the doubt that arises on a quest of certainty, and "God will be!" is the assurance that comes with a quest of understanding. God in time is "God with us"(Matthew 1:23) for "faith seeking understanding." There is a waiting on God that is implied in "God will be!" It is there in Rilke's concluding story of God, "I felt that He was—at some time once was . . . Now—now I sometimes think: He will be . . . Well, this time we'll really wait until it happens."[30] And it is there in T. S. Eliot's lines,

> I said to my soul, be still, and wait . . .
> So the darkness shall be the light,
> and the stillness the dancing.[31]

"Where is the dancing? Where is the way?" Those are the questions of time in one of Ursula LeGuin's stories.[32] If we ask the questions of eternity, "Where do you come from? Where are you going?" and put them alongside the questions of time, then the meaning of time comes to light, "a changing image of eternity." If I see my life as a journey with God in time, then God is not simply at the beginning and the end but all along the way. *There* is the way, *there* is the dancing. "The love is from God and of God and toward God," the words of the old Bedouin to Lawrence of Arabia, imply as much, not only "from God" and "toward God" but also "of God." If I see my own life story as a journey with God in time, I can see the larger story that way as well. God is there at every point on the great circle, therefore, even at the far point where "love must pass through loneliness."

If we pass now from what we can tell to what we can know, from story to relationship, we come to what Martin Buber calls "the realm of unconditional relation." Speaking of "the saying of *I* by Jesus" in his essay *I and Thou*, Buber says "it is the *I* of unconditional relation in which the man calls his *Thou* Father in such a way that he himself is simply Son, and nothing else but Son."[33] As I understand it then, to follow Christ is to enter into that unconditional relation, as Jesus says to Mary Magdalen, "my Father and your Father, my God and your God" (John 20:17). It is to make his Father my Father, to make his God my God. Eternal life thus is to live in that unconditional relationship with God. "You can have a personal relation with the Absolute," as my Vietnamese friend said, a convert from Buddhism to Christianity. "You can be a friend of God, even a lover of God."

There is a great circle of life in Rilke's *Duino Elegies*, like the circulation of the blood, a great circle of life and light and love. "Thus we live," he says, "forever taking leave," *So leben wir und nehmen immer Abschied.*[34] A life living on both sides of death is what he is affirming even in this most famous sentence, the last of the Eighth Elegy, where he is saying all things must pass. That is the paradox of eternal life, the paradox of eternal consciousness. "Death is the side of life that is turned away from, and unillumined by us," he says: "we must try to achieve the greatest possible consciousness of our being, which is at home in both these immeasurable realms and is nourished inexhaustibly by both."[35] Eternal consciousness thus is "the greatest possible consciousness of our being." It is a relationship with God to whom all are alive, as Jesus argues with the Sadducees, "for all live unto him" (Luke 20:38).

There is always a relationship of the living and the dead in every human society, and in his *Duino Elegies* Rilke is seeking to formulate the relationship in such a way that the dead are alive. Whitehead formulates it as "the appropriation of the dead by the living,"[36] but his idea of living on in God's memory is close to the idea of the God of the living to whom the dead are alive. The dead are in our human memory, but if they are also in the divine memory you could say they are alive indeed. I think of the story of Enoch, "And Enoch walked with God; and he was not, for God took him" (Genesis 5:24). To be "oned with God," that is eternal life.

Christ is alive and lives in us—so it is for the follower of Christ. To be alive in us, to be alive in God, is this only to be alive in memory, and is that really to be alive? "Memory is not what the heart desires," Tolkien says.[37] If we see Christ in us and us in God as presences, as "real presences," then it is really to be alive. Parousia is the presence of Christ, as in "I am with you always, even unto the end of the world" (Matthew

28:20). The first meaning of the Greek word *parousia* is "presence," the second is "coming." Eternal life, I believe, belongs to those who live in the presence, and eternal consciousness is an awareness of "real presences," our real presence to one another and to ourselves and to God, and God's real presence to us.

Song Cycle

A Tension of Essences

Eternal life belongs
to those who live
in the Presence,
not just in the present,
for the human being
is incarnate spirit,
passing over
and returning
to itself in God,
through death to life,
through dark to light,
through loneliness to love,
always going home,
going home to God.

An Inner Landscape

Inscape in us
is inner landscape
opening onto infinity,

and centering
around the center
of a stillness
surrounded by a silence,
God's presence
all around
our deepest self,
the quiet eye,
unmoving,
of a moving storm,
a changing image of eternity.

Matter Situates

We are incarnate spirit,
and our brain situates our mind,
our body situates our soul,
and matter is a dimension,
as is time,
and as heighth and breadth
and depth of space,
and thus our brain,
situating words
in one hemisphere
and music in the other,
is a theatre
of music and memory.

An Inner Sea

We listen to our inmost selves
—and do not know
which sea we hear
murmuring
—a sea of presence

but of whom?
of those others
who belong to our lives?
of our presence to ourselves?
of God's presence? as we pray
May I know me!
May I know thee!
in our unknowing
to be oned with God.

A Leap of Mind

A leap of mind
in the eternal
breaking out into sound,
that is song
of the memory
of moments of exaltation
inside of words
inside of music,
emotion recollected
in tranquillity,
and insight into images
of willingness and hope,
catching light
with heart's desire.

The Great Word

Earth, sky
and gods and mortals
—What can free us
from mortality?
but words, the words
of everlasting life,

words of the Word
in the beginning,
spoken in the flesh,
remembered in the spirit
in our storytelling
and our singing
memory and understanding
and our willing one thing.

Eternal Consciousness

If there were no eternal
consciousness in us,
what would life be
but desperation?
That is why there is
this quiet desperation,
but if there is eternal life,
we come to it
by recollection
and by insight into images
of lapsing time
seen in the light
of a promise
of everlasting happiness.

a note on mind and matter

"There's no art to find the mind's construction in the face," Shake-speare says.[1] There is no art, that is, of finding what is going on in the mind from the face. There is no art of finding what is going on in the mind from the brain, we could say too. "While I was speaking to him I did not know what was going on in his head," Wittgenstein quotes from ordinary conversation and comments "In saying this, one is not thinking of brain-processes, but of thought-processes."[2] If we say mind = brain like Nicholas Humphrey in *Seeing Red,*[3] that would mean that brain-processes and thought-processes are one and the same. I want to say instead that mind/brain = spirit/matter where spirit "returns to itself," as Hegel says, and is "pure self-identity within otherness."[4]

What then is matter? I want to say matter is a dimension, like time, and like the dimensions of space. I think this is an implication of Einstein's General Theory of Relativity, just as time as a dimension is an implication of his Special Theory of Relativity. I don't think I am equipped to work this out mathematically as Minkowski did with time, but I imagine the mathematics of it would look something like Riemann's formula in his Inaugural Lecture,[5] a formula that reappears in Einstein's General Theory of Relativity:

$$ds = \sqrt{\Sigma} dx^2 / (1 + \alpha/4 \ \Sigma x^2)$$

It is the formula for the line element ds of a manifold where α is the curvature due to matter and x_1 and x_2 and x_3 are the spatial dimensions, and $x_4 = ict$ is the time dimension, where i is $\sqrt{-1}$ and c is the velocity of light and t is time, and $x_5 = h/mv$ is the matter dimension on the quantum level, the DeBroglie wave length where h is the quantum constant and m is mass and v is velocity. There is the large and the small here. The large is α the curvature due to large masses like the earth and the sun. The small is x_5 the DeBroglie wave length $\lambda = h/mv$.

"Nobody knows," Alain Aspect says in his introduction to Bell's papers, "whether there is a hypothetical limit beyond which decoherence would be inevitable, or whether we always can, at least in principle, take sufficient precautions to protect the system agianst perturbations, no matter how large it is. A clear answer to that question would have immense consequences, both conceptually and for future quantum technologies."[6] If we think of matter as a dimension, like the dimensions of space and time, we can describe matter on the microscopic level in terms of the DeBroglie wave length and on the macroscopic level in terms of the curvature of space. Superposition of states is possible then when the curvature is zero ($\alpha = 0$), but if the curvature is positive ($\alpha > 0$) or negative ($\alpha < 0$), then decoherence sets in.

notes

Bible quotations are from the Revised Standard Version or, in a few cases, the King James Bible.

Preface

1. Leo Tolstoy, *War and Peace,* trans. Louise and Aylmer Maude (New York: Simon & Schuster, 1970), pp. 301–302.

2. Søren Kierkegaard, *Fear and Trembling* (with *Sickness unto Death*), trans. Walter Lowrie (New York: Doubleday Anchor, 1954), p. 30.

3. Albert Bates Lord, *The Singer of Tales,* ed. Stephen Mitchell and Gregory Nagy (Cambridge, Mass.: Harvard University Press, 2003), p. 97, and *The Singer Resumes the Tale,* ed. Mary Louise Lord (Ithaca, N.Y.: Cornell University Press, 1995), pp. 49 and 62.

4. Michael Polanyi, *The Tacit Dimension* (Gloucester, Mass.: Peter Smith, 1983), p. 4.

5. Dag Hammarskjöld, *A Room of Quiet: the United Nations Meditation Room* (New York: United Nations, 1971).

6. Blaise Pascal, *Pensées* #139 (ed. Brunschvicg) in Pascal, *Oeuvres Completes,* ed. Jacques Chevalier (Paris: Editions Gallimard, 1954), pp. 1138–1139.

7. Ludwig Wittgenstein, *Tractatus Logico-Philosophicus,* trans. C. K. Ogden (Mineola, N.Y.: Dover, 1998), p. 106 (#6.4311).

8. Plato, *Timaeus* 37 (my translation).

9. Dag Hammarskjöld, *Markings,* trans. Leif Sjöberg and W. H. Auden (New York: Knopf, 1964), p. 89.

10. Martin Buber, *Ecstatic Confessions*, ed. Paul Mendes-Flohr, trans. Esther Cameron (San Francisco: Harper & Row, 1985), p. 11.

11. Saint Augustine, *Confessions*, trans. Henry Chadwick (Oxford: Oxford University Press, 1991), p. 3 (book 1, chapter 1).

12. Meister Eckhart quoted by Heidegger in his essay on "The Thing" in his *Poetry, Language, Thought*, trans. Albert Hofstadter (New York: Harper & Row, 1971), p. 176.

13. From *The Cloud of Unknowing and Other Works*, trans. Clifton Wolters (New York: Penguin, 1978), pp. 46 and 211.

14. T. E. Lawrence, *Seven Pillars of Wisdom* (Harmondsworth, U.K.: Penguin and Jonathan Cape, 1971), p. 364. See my discussion in my *Reasons of the Heart* (New York: Macmillan, 1978; pbk. Notre Dame, Ind.: University of Notre Dame Press, 1979), p. 1.

15. Henry David Thoreau, *Walden*, ed. J. Lyndon Shanley (Princeton, N.J.: Princeton University Press, 1971), p. 8.

"We can know more than we can tell"

1. Patricia McKillip, *The Sorceress and the Cygnet* (New York: Ace, 1991), p. 92.

2. Michael Polanyi, *The Tacit Dimension*, p. 4.

3. Ursula K. LeGuin, *A Fisherman of the Inland Sea* (New York: Harper Prism, 1994), p. 159.

4. John Henry Newman, *A Grammar of Assent* (Notre Dame, Ind.: University of Notre Dame Press, 1979), p. 276.

5. *The Cloud of Unknowing and Other Works*, (Wolters), p. 46. The title in Middle English is "a book of contemplation, the which is called *The Cloud of Unknowing*, in the which a soul is oned with God."

6. Dag Hammarskjöld, *A Room of Quiet: The United Nations Meditation Room*, opening sentence.

7. Sylvia Shaw Judson, *The Quiet Eye: A Way of Looking at Pictures* (Washington, D.C.: Regnery Gateway, 1982). William Wordsworth, "A Poet's Epitaph," in R. S. Thomas, *A Choice of Wordsworth's Verse* (London: Faber & Faber, 1971), p. 54.

8. Saint Augustine, *Confessions*, (Chadwick), p. 230 (book 11, chapter 14).

9. Alan Lightman, *Einstein's Dreams* (New York: Pantheon, 1993).

10. Martin Heidegger, *The Concept of Time*, trans. William McNeill (Oxford: Blackwell, 1992), p. 22E.

11. Heidegger, *Being and Time,* trans. John Macquarrie and Edward Robinson (New York: Harper, 1962), p. 311.

12. Ibid., p. 19.

13. Saint Augustine, *Confessions* (Chadwick), p. 242 (book 11, chapter 27). Heidegger, *The Concept of Time* (McNeill), pp. 5E–6E.

14. Hammarskjöld, *Markings,* (Sjöberg and Auden), p. 89.

15. George Steiner, *Martin Heidegger* (Chicago: University of Chicago Press, 1991), pp. 15, 131, and 146.

16. Karl Jaspers, *Socrates, Buddha, Confucius, Jesus* (New York: Harcourt, 1962).

17. Rilke quoted in the epigraph of Peter Matthiessen's *Snow Leopard* (New York: Viking, 1978).

18. Albert Schweitzer, *The Quest of the Historical Jesus* (Baltimore: Johns Hopkins University Press, 1998).

19. Henry Clarke Warren, "Introductory Note" to "Buddhist Writings" in *Sacred Writings* (vol. 2) in The Harvard Classics, vol. 45 (New York: Collier, 1910), p. 588.

20. Robert A. F. Thurman, *Inside Tibetan Buddhism,* ed. Barbara Roether (San Francisco: HarperCollins, 1995), p. 15.

21. Matthiessen, *The Snow Leopard,* p. 82 and p. 276.

22. Last words of Gotama to his disciples quoted by Bruce Chatwin, *The Songlines* (New York: Penguin, 1988), p. 179.

23. See the chapter "The Sense of 'I' in Christianity" in my *Peace of the Present* (Notre Dame, Ind.: University of Notre Dame Press, 1991), pp. 92–93.

24. Schweitzer, *The Quest of the Historical Jesus,* p. 403.

25. See Bernard Lonergan, *Method in Theology* (New York: Herder and Herder, 1972), pp. 35, 41, 51, 104, 111 on "self-transcendence."

26. Schweitzer, *The Quest of the Historical Jesus,* p. 403.

27. Ibid., pp. 370–371.

28. Ibid., p. 403.

29. Shakespeare, *The Tempest,* act 1, scene 1, lines 19–25 quoted as the epigraph to my book *The Peace of the Present,* p. vii.

30. Carrin Dunne, *Calming the Storm: Exercises Leading to Contemplation* (Springfield, Ill.: Templegate, 1994).

31. Ludwig Wittgenstein, *Tractatus Logico-Philosophicus,* trans. (Ogden), p. 106 (#6.4311). The other translation I am quoting here is by D. F. Pears and B. F. McGuinness (London: Routledge and Kegan Paul, 1961), p. 147.

32. Isak Dinesen (Karen Blixen), *Last Tales* (New York: Vintage/Random House, 1975), p. 100.

33. Wittgenstein, *Tractatus* (Ogden), p. 108 (#7 concluding sentence).

34. The words of the old Bedouin to Lawrence of Arabia quoted as the starting point of my *Reasons of the Heart*, p. 1.

35. E.M. Forster, *Howard's End* (New York: Holmes and Meier, 1972), pp. 183–184.

36. Robert Bolt, *A Man for All Seasons* (New York: Vintage/Random House, 1962), p. xiii.

37. John Henry Newman, *An Essay on the Development of Christian Doctrine*, ed. J.M. Cameron (Baltimore: Penguin, 1974), p. 114. He is quoting from one of his University Sermons. See my discussion in my *Love's Mind* (Notre Dame, Ind.: University of Notre Dame Press, 1993), p. 9.

38. Shakespeare, *1 Henry IV,* act 2, scene 4, lines 358–359. See my discussion in my *Love's Mind,* p. 63.

39. Saint Augustine, *Soliloquies,* bilingual ed. by Thomas F. Gilligan (New York: Cosmopolitan, 1943), p. 70 (book 2, chapter 1) (my translation of *noverim me! noverim te!*).

40. See Christopher Norris and Andrew Benjamin, *What Is Deconstruction?* (New York and London: Academy Editions/St. Martin's Press, 1988), pp. 7–10 on "the metaphysics of presence." And see George Steiner, *Real Presences* (Chicago: University of Chicago Press, 1989) for an answer.

41. Franz Kafka, *The Great Wall of China,* trans. by Willa and Edwin Muir (New York: Schocken, 1970), p. 183 (#101).

42. Walter Benjamin, *Illuminations,* ed. Hannah Arendt, trans. Harry Zohn (New York: Schocken, 1985), p. 134. See Nicolas Malebranche, *Oeuvres,* ed. Genevieve Rodes-Lewis and Germain Malbreil (Paris: Gallimard, 1979), vol. 1, p. 1132.

43. René Descartes, *A Discourse on Method* (along with *Meditations on First Philosophy* and the *Principles of Philosophy*), trans. John Veitch (London: Everyman/J.M. Dent, 1997), p. 20.

44. Martin Buber, *I and Thou,* trans. Ronald Gregor Smith (New York: Scribner's, 1958), pp. 66–67.

45. Brother Lawrence of the Resurrection (Nicolas Herman), *The Practice of the Presence of God,* ed. Conrad DeMeester, trans. Salvatore Sciurba (Washington, D.C.: Institute of Carmelite Studies, 1994).

46. Jean-Pierre de Caussade, *Abandonment to Divine Providence,* trans. John Beevers (New York: Image/Doubleday, 1975).

47. Simone Weil, *Waiting for God,* trans. Emma Craufurd (New York: Harper Colophon, 1973), p. 105.

48. Saint Thomas Aquinas, *Summa Theologiae* (Rome: Editiones Paulinae, 1962), p. 1426 (II–II q. 83 a.1).

49. John Henry Newman, *Prose and Poetry*, ed. George N. Shuster (New York: Allyn and Bacon, 1925), p. 116.

50. Newman, *Apologia pro Vita Sua* (London: Oxford University Press, 1964), pp. 35–36.

51. Leo Tolstoy, *The Death of Ivan Ilych and Other Stories*, trans. Aylmer Maude (New York: Signet/New American, 1960), p. 156.

52. J. R. R. Tolkien, *The Lord of the Rings*, one-volume ed. (London: George Allen & Unwin, 1976), p. 397 and p. 747.

53. Newman, *Apologia*, p. 203.

54. Pierre Hadot, *The Inner Citadel*, trans. Michael Chase (Cambridge, Mass.: Harvard University Press, 1998).

55. Saint Augustine, *Confessions* (Chadwick), p. 179 (book 10, opening sentence).

56. *The Cloud of Unknowing* (Wolters), p. 105 (chapters 37 and 38).

57. Dilbert R. Hillers in his foreword (1998) to Schweitzer, *The Quest of the Historical Jesus*, p. xiv. Schweitzer repeats the words of his conclusion here later in his autobiography, *Out of My Life and Thought*, trans. A. B. Lemke (New York: Henry Holt, 1990), pp. 58–59.

58. Rudolf Otto, *Mysticism East and West*, trans. Bertha L. Bracey and Richenda C. Payne (New York: Macmillan, 1960).

Is Matter a Dimension?

1. Padraic Colum, *Storytelling New and Old* (New York: Macmillan, 1968), p. 4.

2. Max Jacob in his preface (1916) to his prose poems *The Dice Cup*, ed. Michael Brownstein (New York: State University of New York, 1979), p. 5. See my discussion in my *Mystic Road of Love* (Notre Dame, Ind.: University of Notre Dame Press, 1999), "A Note on the Dante-Riemann Universe," pp. 137–141, where I propose this idea that matter is a dimension.

3. Heinrich von Kleist in *Essays on Dolls*, trans. Idris Parry and Paul Kegan (New York: Syrens/Penguin, 1994), p. 3 (the essay is on pp. 1–12).

4. Ibid., p. 12.

5. Ibid., p. 7.

6. Bruce Chatwin, *The Songlines*, p. 176.

7. Wittgenstein, *Tractatus* (Ogden), p. 103 (#6.3611).

8. Kleist in *Essays on Dolls*, p. 6.

9. Wittgenstein, *Philosophical Investigations*, 3rd ed., trans. G. E. M. Anscombe (Englewood Cliffs, N.J.: Prentice Hall, 1975), p. 127 (#427).

10. Yirmiyahu Yovel, *Hegel's Preface to the Phenomenology of Spirit*, trans. and commentary (Princeton, N.J.: Princeton University Press, 2005), p. 170.

11. The translation is from Thomas Gilby, *Saint Thomas Aquinas: Philosophical Texts* (New York: Oxford University Press, 1960), pp. 2 and 3. The Latin is *canticum autem exultatio mentis de aeternis habita, prorumpens in vocem*, "song is exultation of the mind upon eternal things, breaking into sound" (or "into voice"). See my discussion in my *Road of the Heart's Desire* (Notre Dame, Ind.: University of Notre Dame Press, 2002), p. 87.

12. Aniruddh Patel in *Brain Matters* (San Diego: Neurosciences Institute, Fall 2005).

13. See my *Love's Mind*, p. 136.

14. See above, note 6.

15. E. M. Forster, *Howard's End* (New York: Knopf, 1991), p. 32 (opening of chapter 5).

16. Plato, *Timaeus* 37D (my translation).

17. Isak Dinesen (Karen Blixen), *Last Tales* (New York: Vintage/ Random House, 1975), p. 26.

18. Søren Kierkegaard, *Fear and Trembling* (with *Sickness unto Death*), trans. Walter Lowrie (New York: Doubleday Anchor, 1954), p. 30.

19. Shakespeare, 1 Henry IV quoted above in the first chapter, note 38.

20. Paul Valery, *Introduction to the Method of Leonardo da Vinci*, trans. Thomas McGreevy (London: John Rodker, 1929), especially pp. 9 and 32. See my discussion in my *Love's Mind*, p. 61.

21. Monica Strauss, *Leonardo da Vinci* (New York: Artist's Limited Edition, 1984), p. 5.

22. Wassily Kandinsky quoted as epigraph by Thomas Habinek, *The World of Roman Song* (Baltimore: Johns Hopkins University Press, 2005), p. 1.

23. Michel Serres, *Genesis*, trans. Genevieve James and James Nielson (Ann Arbor, Mich.: University of Michigan Press, 1995).

24. Martin Buber, *Ecstatic Confessions*, p. 11.

25. George Eliot, *Middlemarch* (Oxford: Oxford University Press, 1996), p. 182 (chapter 20).

26. Walter Pater, *The Renaissance* (New York: Macmillan, 1900), p. 140 ("The School of Giorgione").

27. Wittgenstein, *Tractatus* (Ogden), p. 107 (#6.522).

28. Monica Strauss, *Leonardo da Vinci*, p. 27.

29. James Hillman, *The Thought of the Heart* (Eranos Lectures) (Dallas, Tex.: Spring Publications, 1981), p. 24.

30. W. B. Yeats, *Mythologies*, ending with his essay *Per Amica Silentia Lunae* (1917) divided into two parts, *Anima Hominis* and *Anima Mundi* (New York: Collier-Macmillan, 1959), pp. 317–369. T. S. Eliot's critique is called *After Strange Gods* (London: Faber & Faber, 1934).

31. Wittgenstein, *Philosophical Investigations*, p. 178.

32. Le Corbusier, *The Modulor* ("A harmonious measure to the human scale, universally applicable to architecture and mechanics") (Basel and Boston: Birkhauser, 2000).

33. William Harvey, *De Motu Cordis*, trans. Chauncey D. Leake (Springfield, Ill.: Charles C. Thomas, 1970), p. 5.

34. Martin Heidegger, *Discourse on Thinking*, a trans. of *Gelassenheit* by John M. Anderson and E. Hans Freund (New York: Harper & Row, 1959), p. 55.

35. See my discussion of problem and mystery in my *City of the Gods* (New York: Macmillan, 1965; pbk. Notre Dame, Ind.: University of Notre Dame Press, 1978), p. 4.

36. Kleist, "The Marionette Theatre" in *Essays on Dolls* (Parry), p. 12.

37. Saint Thérèse of Lisieux, *The Story of a Soul*, trans. John Clarke (Washington, D.C.: Institute of Carmelite Studies, 1976).

38. Colum, *Storytelling New and Old*, p. 4.

39. Saint Thérèse, *The Story of a Soul*, p. 214.

40. Ibid., p. 211.

41. Saint John of the Cross, *Dark Night of the Soul*, trans. and ed. E. Allison Peers (New York: Doubleday/Image, 1990), p. 34.

42. William James, *The Will to Believe* along with *Human Immortality* (New York: Dover, 1956, a reprint of the 1897 edition of the one and the 1898 edition of the other).

43. Dag Hammarskjöld, *A Room of Quiet: The United Nations Meditation Room*, opening and closing sentences.

44. Yovel's translation of Hegel quoted above in note 10.

45. Meister Eckhart quoted by William James, *The Varieties of Religious Experience* (New York: Mentor, 1958), p. 320.

The epigraph is from Martin Buber, *Ecstatic Confessions*, p. 11.

1. See Christopher Norris and Andrew Benjamin, *What Is Decon-struction?* (London and New York: Academy Editions/St. Martin's Press, 1988), pp. 7–10 ("The Metaphysics of Presence").

2. George Steiner, *Real Presences* (Chicago: University of Chicago Press, 1989).

3. Elie Wiesel, *The Trial of God,* trans. Marion Wiesel (New York: Schocken, 1986), pp. 63–64.

4. Franz Kafka, *The Great Wall of China,* trans. Willa and Edwin Muir (New York: Schocken, 1974), p. 183.

5. Giambattista Vico, *New Science,* trans. David Marsh (New York: Penguin, 1999), book 2: Poetic Wisdom, pp. 135–351.

6. Aristotle, *Poetics* 1451b in *The Basic Works of Aristotle,* ed. Rich-ard McKeon (New York: Random House, 1941), p. 1464.

7. Kathleen Norris, *Dakota* (New York: Ticknor & Fields, 1993), p. 102.

8. Saint Augustine, *Confessions,* (Chadwick), p. 191 (book 10, chapter 14).

9. John Henry Newman, *Apologia pro Vita Sua* (London: Oxford University Press, 1964), p. 247.

10. James Robert Goetsch, Jr., *Vico's Axioms* (New Haven, Conn.: Yale University Press, 1995), p. 139.

11. Ibid., p. 138.

12. Newman, *Apologia,* pp. 294–295.

13. Goetsch, *Vico's Axioms,* p. 139. And see pp. 81–87 on "the invin-cible enthymeme."

14. Richard Wilhelm and Cary F. Baynes (trans.), *The I Ching or Book of Changes,* 3rd ed. (Princeton, N.J.: Princeton University Press, 1967), p. 184 (#47).

15. C.S. Lewis, *Surprised by Joy* (San Diego: Harcourt Brace Jova-novich, 1955), pp. 17–18.

16. Karl Jaspers, *The Perennial Scope of Philosophy,* trans. Ralph Manheim (New York: Philosophical Library, 1949), p. 30.

17. C.S. Lewis, *Surprised by Joy,* p. 238.

18. Martin Lings, *A Sufi Saint of the Twentieth Century* (Lahore, Pakistan: Suhail Academy, 1981), p. 210 ("Whoso setteth out for God reacheth him not, but whoso leaneth upon him for support is not un-aware of him").

19. The actor Peter Sellers quoted on his official website.

20. Goethe, *Eckermann Gesprache mit Goethe* (Frankfurt am Main: Deutscher Klassiker Verlag, 1999), p. 350 (April 10, 1829) (Ich kenne mich auch nicht und Gott soll mich auch davor behuten).

21. Henry Chadwick in his introduction to Saint Augustine, *Confessions*, p. xii.

22. Igor Stravinsky, *Symphony of Psalms* (London: Boosey & Hawkes, 1948), where the three psalms in the RSV are Psalm 38:13 and 14, Psalm 39:2–4, and Psalm 150. On the Psalms in Saint Augustine's *Confessions* see Henry Chadwick's introduction, p. xxii.

23. Max Frisch, *I'm Not Stiller,* trans. Michael Bullock (New York: Random House/Vintage, 1958), p. 372.

24. Kierkegaard, *The Sickness unto Death* (with *Fear and Trembling*), p. 147.

25. Ray Bradbury, *Dandelion Wine* (New York: Bantam, 1969), p. 7.

26. See Gareth Matthews' introduction to Saint Augustine, *On the Trinity,* trans. Stephen McKenna (Cambridge: Cambridge University Press, 2002), p. xxvi (the two passages in Augustine are *On the Trinity,* book 15, chapter 12, and *City of God,* book 11, chapter 26).

27. Isak Dinesen, *Last Tales*, p. 26.

28. Bernard Lonergan, *De Constitutione Christi* (Rome: Gregorian, 1956), pp. 131–145. See also his Aquinas Lecture, *The Subject* (Milwaukee: Marquette University Press, 1968) on his concept of the subject.

29. Michael Gazzaniga, *The Mind's Past* (Berkeley: University of California Press, 1998), p. 1.

30. I have been unable to locate this quotation from Irving Howe.

31. Kierkegaard, *Fear and Trembling* quoted above in chapter 2, note 18.

32. Wittgenstein, *Tractatus* (Ogden), p. 106 (#6.4311).

33. See Martin Heidegger, "Hegel's Concept of Experience" in Heidegger, *Off the Beaten Track,* ed. and trans. Julian Young and Kenneth Haynes (Cambridge: Cambridge University Press, 2002), pp. 86ff.

34. Pascal, *Pensées* #139 (ed. Brunschvicg) from Pascal, *Oeuvres Completes,* ed. Jacques Chevalier (Paris: Gallimard, 1954), pp. 1138–1139.

35. Bernard Lonergan, *Insight* (London/New York: Longmans Green, 1957), p. xxviii.

36. Mimi Louise Haskins as quoted by George VI in a Christmas broadcast in 1939, *King George VI to His Peoples* (London: John Murray, 1952), p. 21.

37. Reiner Schurmann, *Wandering Joy: Meister Eckhart's Mystical Philosophy* (translations and commentary) (Great Barrington, Mass.: Lindisfarne, 2001), p. xx.

38. Rainer Maria Rilke, *The Notebooks of Malte Laurids Brigge,* trans. M. D. Herter Norton (New York: Norton, 1964), p. 209.

39. Henry Vaughan, "The World" and "They Are All Gone into the World of Light" in Robert Penn Warren and Albert Erskine, eds., *Six Centuries of Great Poetry* (New York: Bantam Doubleday Dell, 1955), pp. 271 and 276.

40. Martin Buber, *I and Thou,* p. xv.

41. Christopher Smart, *Jubilate Agno* in Karina Williamson, ed. *The Poetical Works of Christopher Smart,* vol.1 (Oxford: Clarendon, 1980), pp. 4 and 53. Benjamin Britten set these words to music in *Rejoice in the Lamb,* opus 30 (1943). See my discussion in my *Church of the Poor Devil* (New York, Macmillan/Notre Dame, Ind.: University of Notre Dame Press, 1982), pp. 122–123.

42. Patricia A. McKillip, *The Moon and the Face* (New York: Berkeley, 1985), p. 88.

43. Kierkegaard, *Fear and Trembling,* p. 30, and *Sickness unto Death,* p. 163.

44. Einstein quoted by Abraham Pais, *Subtle is the Lord . . .* (Oxford: Oxford University Press, 1982), p. 468.

45. Kierkegaard, *Concluding Unscientific Postsript,* trans. David F. Swenson and Walter Lowrie (Princeton: Princeton University Press, 1941), p. 97.

46. Rilke, *Stories of God,* trans. M. D. Herter Norton (New York: Norton, 1963), p. 29.

47. John S. Dunne, *A Search for God in Time and Memory* (New York: Macmillan, 1969; pbk. Notre Dame, Ind.: University of Notre Dame Press, 1977).

48. Eric R. Kandel, *In Search of Memory: The Emergence of a New Science of Mind* (New York: Norton, 2006).

49. Nicolas Malebranche, *Oeuvres,* ed. Genevieve Rodis-Lewis and Germain Malbreil (Paris: Gallimard, 1979), vol. 1, p. 1152. See my discussion in *Love's Mind,* pp. 86–87, and *Reading the Gospel* (Notre Dame, Ind.: University of Notre Dame Press, 2000), pp. 7, 11–12, 74, 100, and 129.

50. Walter Benjamin, *Illuminations,* ed. Hannah Arendt and trans. Harry Zohn (New York: Schocken, 1985), p. 134. Paul Celan, *Collected Prose,* trans. Rosmarie Waldrop (London: Carcanet, 1986), p. 50.

51. See the chapter "Attention Must Be Paid" in Kandel, *In Search of Memory*, pp. 307–316.

52. See George Steiner, *Martin Heidegger* (Chicago: University of Chicago Press, 1991), pp. 34–35 on this question in Leibniz and in Heidegger.

53. S.M. Barrett, ed., *Geronimo: His Own Story* (New York: Dutton, 1970).

54. Saint Augustine, *Confessions* (Chadwick), p. 201 (book 10, chapter 27).

55. See Heidegger, *The Concept of Time*, trans. William McNeill (Oxford: Blackwell, 1992), p. 22E. See my discussion in my *Vision Quest* (Notre Dame, Ind.: University of Notre Dame Press, 2006), pp. 24–33.

56. See my discussion in *A Search for God in Time and Memory*, pp. 197–198 (referring to Bede, *Ecclesiastical History*, II, 13).

57. Ray Bradbury, *Dandelion Wine*, p. 7.

58. See Mitzi Brunsdale, *James Herriot* (New York: Twayne, 1997).

59. Saint Augustine, *On the Trinity*, ed. Gareth Matthews, trans. Stephen McKenna (Cambridge: Cambridge University Press, 2002), pp. 190–191 (book 15, chapter 12). See Gareth Matthews' Introduction, p. xxvi, where he also refers to *The City of God*, book 11, chapter 26.

60. Kierkegaard, *Sickness unto Death* (Lowrie), p. 146.

61. Erwin Schrodinger, *What Is Life?* and *Mind and Matter* and *Autobiographical Sketches* (Cambridge: Cambridge University Press, 1967).

62. James D. Watson, Foreword to *The Human Genome*, ed. Carina Dennis and Richard Gallagher (New York: Palgrave, 2001), p. 7.

63. *Evolution and Molecular Biology: Scientific Perspectives on Divine Action*, ed. Robert John Russell, William R. Stoeger, and Francisco J. Ayala (Vatican City State: Vatican Observatory; Berkeley, Calif.: Center for Theology and the Natural Sciences, 1998).

64. Tolkien, *Lord of the Rings*, p. 1122.

65. Kant, *Critique of Pure Reason*, trans. F. Max Muller (New York: Doubleday Anchor, 1966), p. 515.

66. Buber, *I and Thou* (Ronald Gregor Smith), pp. 66–67.

67. See above, note 36.

68. Heraclitus, Fragment #18 in Kathleen Freeman, *Ancilla to the Pre-Socratic Philosophers* (Cambridge, Mass.: Harvard University Press, 1957), p. 26.

69. Jean Giono, *The Man Who Planted Trees*, afterword by Norma L. Goodrich (Chelsea, Ver.: Chelsea Green, 1985), p. 50.

Words and Music

1. I ended *A Vision Quest* with this quotation (p. 117). Here it is a starting point.

2. See my discussion of the Latin above in chapter 2, at note 11.

3. See my discussion of Kant's problem and Wittgenstein's solution (*Tractatus* 6.36111) in *A Vision Quest*, p. 37.

4. See my discussion of Vico's idea on that same page.

5. See my discussion of Beethoven's theme in the round and the string quartet in *The Music of Time* (Notre Dame, Ind.: University of Notre Dame Press, 1996), pp. 81–82.

6. Kierkegaard, *Fear and Trembling* (Lowrie), pp. 51–52.

7. Ibid., p. 52.

8. Saint Augustine, *Confessions* (Chadwick), p. 191 (book 10, chapter 14).

9. Kierkegaard, *The Concept of Dread*, trans. Walter Lowrie (Princeton, N.J.: Princeton University Press, 1957), p. 139 (title of the last chapter).

10. Kierkegaard, *Fear and Trembling* (Lowrie), p. 59.

11. Steven Mithen, *The Singing Neanderthals* (Cambridge, Mass.: Harvard University Press, 2006).

12. Claude Levi-Strauss, *Myth and Meaning* (New York: Schocken, 1995), p. 52.

13. M. Owen Lee, *Wagner's Ring* (New York: Limelight Editions, 1998), p. 113.

14. Inayat Khan (1882–1927) quoted by Bod Snyder as the epigraph of his book *Music and Memory* (Cambridge, Mass.: MIT Press, 2000), p. xiii.

15. Lewis Carroll, *Alice in Wonderland* (with *Alice through the Looking Glass*) (New York: Grosset & Dunlap, 1998), pp. 110–111 (chapter 10).

16. Charles O. Hartman, *Jazz Text* (Princeton, N.J.: Princeton University Press, 1991), p. 9. See my discussion in my *Music of Time*, pp. 93ff.

17. W. B. Yeats, *Collected Poems* (New York: Macmillan, 1972), p. 214.

18. See my *Road of the Heart's Desire*, pp. 124–127.

19. See above, Hegel quoted in the second chapter, note 10.

20. See above, Kleist quoted in the same chapter, note 3.

21. See my *Church of the Poor Devil*, p. 130. I am quoting Saint Thomas Aquinas and he is quoting Saint Augustine.

22. Glenn W. Most, *Doubting Thomas* (Cambridge, Mass.: Harvard University Press, 2006).

23. This is a saying I frequently quote but have been unable to find its source.

24. *The Works of George Herbert*, ed. E.E. Hutchinson (Oxford: Clarendon, 1945), p. 354 (*Outlandish Proverbs* 1006).

25. W.B. Yeats, *A Vision* (New York: Collier, 1966), p. 83. See my discussion in my *Music of Time*, p. 12.

26. Heidegger, *The Concept of Time* (McNeill), p. 22E. Quoted above in the first chapter, note 10.

27. Tolkien, *Lord of the Rings*, p. 369.

28. Hopkins, *Poems and Prose* (New York: Knopf, 1995), p. 123.

29. Ibid.

30. Kierkegaard, *Sickness unto Death* (with *Fear and Trembling*) (Lowrie), p. 146.

31. Hopkins, *Poems and Prose*, pp. 123–124.

32. Mithen, *The Singing Neanderthals*, p. 256 (see also p. 16).

33. Jacques Derrida, *Of Spirit: Heidegger and the Question*, trans. Geoffrey Bennington and Rachel Bowley (Chicago: University of Chicago Press, 1987).

34. Tolkien, *Lord of the Rings*, p. 1122.

35. Heidegger, *Discourse on Thinking* (Anderson and Freund), p. 55 (quoted above in the second chapter, note 34).

36. Yovel, *Hegel's Preface to the Phenomenology of Spirit*, p. 170.

37. Saint Thomas and Saint Augustine quoted above at note 21.

38. See my *Music of Time*, p. 78, where I diagram the cycle of fire in terms of "we can know more than we can tell."

39. Rilke, *Stories of God* (Norton), p. 126. And see his sixth *Letter to a Young Poet*.

40. Mithen, *The Singing Neanderthals*, chapter 1 "The mystery of music," pp. 1–10, and chapter 17 "A mystery explained, but not diminished," pp. 266–278.

41. *The Notebooks of Joseph Joubert*, ed. and trans. Paul Auster, with an afterword by Maurice Blanchot, trans. Lydia Davis (San Francisco: North Point Press, 1983), pp. 180–181. See my discussion in my *Music of Time*, p. 15.

42. See my discussion of rest in restlessness in my *Time and Myth* (1973; Notre Dame, Ind.: University of Notre Dame Press, 1975), p. 79.

43. Flaubert wrote three successive versions of *Tentation de Saint Antoine*. See his *Oeuvres Completes*, vol. 1 (Paris: Editions du Seuil,

1964), pp. 375ff. See my discussion in my *Way of All the Earth* (New York: Macmillan, 1972; Notre Dame, Ind.: University of Notre Dame Press, 1978), pp. 34–36.

44. Tolstoy quoted by Max Gorky, *Reminiscences of Tolstoy, Chekhov, and Andreev*, trans. Katherine Mansfield, S.S. Koteliansky, and Leonard Woolf (London: Hogarth, 1948), p. 23. See my discussion in my *Love's Mind*, p. 60.

45. Hopkins, *Poems and Prose*, p. 51.

46. Wittgenstein, *Tractatus* (Ogden), p. 106 (#6.4311).

Story and Song

1. Michel Serres, *Genesis*, trans. Genevieve James and James Nielson (Ann Arbor: University of Michigan Press, 1995), p. 138.

2. See J.R.R. Tolkien, *The Silmarillion*, ed. Christopher Tolkien (Boston: Houghton Mifflin, 1977), pp. 15–17, and C.S. Lewis, *The Magician's Nephew* (New York: Collier Macmillan, 1955), pp. 98–115. See my discussion in my *Vision Quest*, pp. 70–71.

3. Ursula LeGuin, *A Wizard of Earthsea* (New York: Bantam, 2004), p. 164. See my discussion in my *Reading the Gospel*, p. 21.

4. A.N. Whitehead, *Religion in the Making* (New York: Macmillan, 1926), p. 160.

5. Shakespeare, Sonnets 30:2 and 107:2.

6. Shakespeare, *1 Henry IV*, act 2, scene 4, line 359, quoted above in the first chapter at note 38.

7. Henry Vaughan quoted above in the chapter Real Presences, note 39.

8. Albert Bates Lord, *The Singer Resumes the Tale* (Ithaca, N.Y.: Cornell University Press, 1995), p. 62. See ibid., p. 49, and see his earlier work, *The Singer of Tales* (Cambridge, Mass.: Harvard University Press, 1961), p. 97. See my discussion in my *Road of the Heart's Desire*, p. vii and pp. 109–110.

9. Tolkien, *Lord of the Rings*, p. 739.

10. Dunne, *A Journey with God in Time* (Notre Dame, Ind.: University of Notre Dame Press, 2003), p. 27.

11. Paul Valery quoted above in the second chapter, note 20.

12. Martin Buber quoted above in the third chapter, note 40.

13. Walter Benjamin quoting Georg Lukacs in his essay "The Storyteller" in his *Illuminations*, p. 99.

14. George Bernard Shaw, *Back to Methuselah*, quoted by Padraic Colum, *Storytelling New and Old* (New York: Macmillan, 1968), p. 23.

15. Isak Dinesen (Karen Blixen), *Last Tales*, p. 26. See my discussion in my *Church of the Poor Devil*, p. 123, and my *Road of the Heart's Desire*, p. 93.

16. Robert Jay Lifton, *Death in Life* (New York: Random House, 1967), p. 505.

17. Henry David Thoreau, *Walden*, ed. J. Lyndon Shanley (Princeton, N.J.: Princeton University Press, 1971), p. 8.

18. Rilke, *Stories of God* (Norton), p. 126.

19. Pierre Hadot, *Plotinus or the Simplicity of Vision*, trans. Michael Chase (Chicago: University of Chicago Press, 1993).

20. John G. Neihardt, *Black Elk Speaks* (Lincoln: University of Nebraska Press, 1961), pp. 1–2.

21. Ibid., p. 29.

22. Peter Levi, *The Holy Gospel of John* (Wilton, Conn.: Morehouse-Barlow, 1985), p. 7. See my discussion in my *Reading the Gospel*, p. 24.

23. Wendell Berry, "Setting Out" in *The Wheel* (San Francisco: North Point Press, 1982), p. 26.

24. Alcmaeon, Fragment 2, trans. Kathleen Freeman in *Ancilla to the PreSocratic Philosophers* (Cambridge, Mass.: Harvard University Press, 1957), p. 40.

25. T. S. Eliot, *Four Quartets* (San Diego: Harcourt Brace Jovanovich, 1988), pp. 23 and 32 (opening and closing lines of "East Coker").

26. Hermann Broch, *The Death of Virgil*, trans. Jean Starr Untermeyer (New York: Random House/Vintage, 1995), p. 482.

27. The theme of my doctoral dissertation at the Gregorian University in Rome, *Participation in the Theology of Saint Thomas* (Notre Dame, 1958). See the summary in my article "St. Thomas' Theology of Participation" in *Theological Studies*, 1957.

28. Tolstoy, *War and Peace*, trans. Constance Garnett (New York: Random House/Modern Library, n.d.), p. 256 (part three, chapter 16).

29. Paul Griffiths, *A Concise History of Western Music* (Cambridge: Cambridge University Press, 2006). I am quoting here the titles of the eight parts of the book.

30. Ibid., p. 7.

31. Wittgenstein, *Tractatus* (Ogden), p. 106 (#6.4311).

32. See my discussion of this phrase in my *Love's Mind*, p. 99, where I also translate the poem "Dark Night" on pp. 100–101.

33. See my discussion of these phrases "God is dead" and "infinite grief" and "absolute suffering" and "Golgotha of absolute spirit" in my *City of the Gods*, pp. 188–191.

34. James Joyce, *Finnegans Wake* (New York: Viking Press, 1939). I am putting together the closing words "A way a lone a last a loved a long the" and the opening word "riverrun," as they seem intended to make a circle.

35. Shakespeare, Sonnet 107:1–4. I am echoing the opening words of the commentary in *The Complete Works of Shakespeare,* ed. Irving Ribner and George Lyman Kittridge (Waltham, Mass., and Toronto: Xerox College Publishing, 1971), p. 1715.

36. William Blake, *The Marriage of Heaven and Hell* in *The Poetry and Prose of William Blake,* ed. David V. Erdman (New York: Doubleday, 1965), p. 39.

37. Tolstoy, *War and Peace* quoted in the passage cited above in note 28.

38. C. G. Jung, *Answer to Job,* trans. R. F. C. Hull (New York: Meridian, 1960), p. 184.

39. Tolstoy, *War and Peace* (Garnett), p. 915 (part twelve, chapter 16).

40. LeGuin, *A Wizard of Earthsea,* p. 128.

41. Saint Thérèse of Lisieux, *Story of a Soul,* trans. John Clarke (Washington, D.C.: ICS Publications, 1976), p. 213.

42. Nietzsche, *Thus Spake Zarathustra,* trans. Walter Kaufman in *The Portable Nietzsche* (New york: Viking, 1960), p. 395 (part four: The Welcome).

43. Heraclitus quoted above in the third chapter, note 68.

44. Jean Paul Sartre, *L'existentialisme est un humanisme* (Paris: Nagel, 1946), p. 27 ("angoisse, delaissement, desespoir").

45. Hannah Arendt, *Men in Dark Times* (New York: Harcourt, Brace and World, 1968).

Eternal Consciousness

1. Henry David Thoreau, *Walden,* p. 8.

2. Soren Kierkegaard, *Fear and Trembling* (Lowrie), p. 30.

3. The four paintings by Thomas Cole are reproduced in my memoir, *A Journey with God in Time* (Notre Dame, Ind.: University of Notre Dame Press, 2003). The originals are in the National Gallery in Washington, D.C.

4. Albert Lord, *The Singer of Tales,* p. 97, and *The Singer Resumes the Tale,* pp. 49 and 62, quoted in the previous chapter at note 8.

5. Charles Dickens, *A Tale of Two Cities,* ed. Richard Maxwell (New York: Penguin, 2000), p. 5 (opening sentence).

6. Tolkien, *Lord of the Rings*, p. 739.

7. Heidegger, *Discourse on Thinking* (Anderson and Freund), p. 55.

8. Augustine, *On the Trinity*, ed. Gareth Matthews, trans. Stephen McKenna, p. 223.

9. Yovel (trans. and commentary), *Hegel's Preface to the Phenomenology of Spirit*, p. 170.

10. Ludwig Feuerbach quoted in *The Oxford Minidictionary of Quotations* (Oxford: Oxford University Press, 1983), p. 160.

11. Eric R. Kandel, *In Search of Memory*, cited above in the third chapter, note 48.

12. Jonathan D. Spence, *The Memory Palace of Matteo Ricci* (New York: Penguin, 1984).

13. João Ubaldo Ribeiro, *An Invincible Memory* (New York: Harper & Row, 1989), epigraph.

14. Bernard J. F. Lonergan, *Insight: A Study of Human Understanding*.

15. Yovel, *Hegel's Preface to the Phenomenology of Spirit*, p. 170.

16. E. M. Forster, *Howard's End*, pp. 183–184.

17. Hegel quoted by J. B. Baillie in his translator's introduction to Hegel, *Phenomenology of Mind* (London: Allen & Unwin and New York: Macmillan, 1961), p. 16. The quotation from Aristotle on the knowing of knowing is on the Hegel title page.

18. Newman, *Apologia pro Vita Sua* (London: Oxford University Press, 1964), p. 203.

19. Otto Rank, *Beyond Psychology* (New York: Dover, 1958), p. 196.

20. Pierre Hadot, *The Inner Citadel: The Meditations of Marcus Aurelius*, trans. Michael Chase (Cambridge, Mass.: Harvard University Press, 1998).

21. Daniel A. Dombrowski, *Rethinking the Ontological Argument* (Cambridge: Cambridge University Press, 2006).

22. Karl Barth, *Anselm: Fides Quaerens Intellectum*, trans. W. Robertson (Cleveland and New York: Meridian/World, 1962).

23. W. B. Yeats, *A Vision* (New York: Collier, 1966), p. 83.

24. M. Owen Lee, *Wagner's Ring* (New York: Limelight, 1998), p. 113.

25. *Hopkins: Poems and Prose*, p. 123.

26. Hermann Broch, *The Death of Virgil*, trans. Jean Starr Untermeyer (San Francisco: North Point Press, 1945), p. 482.

27. Rilke, *Letters to a Young Poet*, p. 49.

28. Rilke, *Stories of God*, p. 126. See my discussion in *A Search for God in Time and Memory*, pp. 179–205.

29. Kierkegaard, *Philosophical Fragments*, p. 53.

30. Rilke, *Stories of God*, pp. 126–127.

31. T.S. Eliot, *Four Quartets*, p. 28 ("East Coker," lines 123 and 128).

32. Ursula LeGuin, *A Fisherman of the Inland Sea* (New York: Harper Prism, 1995), p. 185.

33. Martin Buber, *I and Thou*, pp. 66–67.

34. Rilke, *Duino Elegies* (bilingual edition) (Berkeley: University of California Press, 1961), p. 64 (German text) (my trans.).

35. Rilke, *Selected Letters 1902–1926*, trans. R.F.C. Hull (London: Macmillan, 1946), pp. 392f. (Letter to Witold von Hulewicz, November 13, 1925).

36. A.N. Whitehead, *Process and Reality* (New York: Macmillan, 1929), p. ix. See my discussion in my *City of the Gods*, p. 21.

37. Tolkien, *Lord of the Rings*, p. 399.

A Note on Mind and Matter

1. Shakespeare, *Macbeth*, act 1, scene 4, lines 11–12 in *The Oxford Shakespeare* (London: Oxford University Press, 1957), p. 849.

2. Wittgenstein, *Philosophical Investigations*, p. 127 (#427).

3. Nicholas Humphrey, *Seeing Red: A Study in Consciousness* (Cambridge, Mass.: Belknap/Harvard, 2006).

4. Yirmiyahu Yovel, *Hegel's Preface to the Phenomenology of Spirit*, p. 170.

5. See my *Mystic Road of Love*, pp. 137–141 ("A Note on the Dante-Riemann Universe").

6. Alain Aspect, introduction to J.S. Bell, *Speakable and Unspeakable in Quantum Mechanics*, 2nd ed. (Cambridge: Cambridge University Press, 2004), p. xxxi.

index of names